FUNDAMENTAL LEGAL CONCEPTIONS AS APPLIED IN JUDICIAL REASONING

BY WESLEY NEWCOMB HOHFELD

Fundamental Legal Conceptions as Applied in Judicial Reasoning

by Wesley Newcomb Hohfeld

Edited by
DAVID CAMPBELL and PHILIP THOMAS
Cardiff Law School

With an Introduction by
NIGEL E. SIMMONDS
Corpus Christi College, Cambridge

Routledge
Taylor & Francis Group
LONDON AND NEW YORK

First published 2001 by Ashgate Publishing

2 Park Square, Milton Park, Abingdon, Oxon OX14 4RN
711 Third Avenue, New York, NY 10017, USA

Routledge is an imprint of the Taylor & Francis Group, an informa business

First issued in paperback 2016

British Library Cataloguing in Publication Data
Hohfeld, Wesley Newcomb
Fundamental legal conceptions as applied in judicial reasoning. - New ed. - (Classical jurisprudence series)
1. Law - Methodology
I. Title II. Campbell, David, 1958- III. Thomas, Philip A.
(Philip Aneurin, 1940-
340.1

Library of Congress Control Number: 2001091406

ISBN 13: 978-1-85521-668-6 (hbk)
ISBN 13: 978-1-138-25471-8 (pbk)

Contents

Preface to the New Edition

Fundamental Legal Conceptions was first published as two articles in (1913) 23 *Yale Law Journal* 16 and (1917) 26 *Yale Law Journal* 710. As he made clear in the first footnote to the second article, Hohfeld intended to publish an expanded version of these articles as a book of the same title. His death in 1918 prevented this. The two articles were, however, published by Yale University Press (in conjunction with Humphrey Milford of London and Oxford University Press) in 1919 as a pamphlet edited by Walter Wheeler Cook entitled *Fundamental Legal Conceptions, As Applied in Judicial Reasoning: And Other Legal Essays*. This pamphlet included some of Hohfeld's intended changes and reprinted Cook's article on 'Hohfeld's Contributions to the Science of Law' (1919) 28 *Yale Law Journal* 721 as an introduction. It was reprinted in 1920. The material contained in the pamphlet was reprinted by Yale University Press in 1923 as a book of the same title which included Hohfeld's other writings. The two essays on 'Fundamental Legal Conceptions' and Cook's introduction have been reprinted a number of times by Yale University Press and, from 1964, a new foreword by Arthur L Corbin was added. The 1964 Yale University Press reprint was reprinted again in 1978 by Greenwood Press of Westport, Connecticut.

For this edition, Cook's introduction and Corbin's foreword have been replaced by a new introduction by Dr Nigel E Simmonds of Corpus Christi College, Cambridge. In addition, the editors have silently corrected obvious errors and have made a number of other minor changes. In all previous editions, the format of, in essence, the *Yale Law Journal* publication was reproduced. In this edition, the page setting of previous editions has been amended to try to improve the clarity of Hohfeld's paragraphing; Hohfeld's and Cook's numbering of the footnotes has been rationalised, in part to incorporate properly Hohfeld's changes; and additional information has been supplied to improve the accuracy of some citations. No material has, however, been omitted from the footnotes.

David Campbell
Philip Thomas
Cardiff Law School

Introduction

by Nigel E Simmonds

Hohfeld's *Fundamental Legal Conceptions* was originally published in the form of two articles in the *Yale Law Journal* for 1913 and 1917. Hohfeld had intended to publish an expanded version of these articles as part of a book, but his death prevented the completion of the project.

Little seems to be known about Hohfeld beyond his published work. Born in 1879, he studied chemistry before turning to law and it has been suggested that his approach to analytical jurisprudence resembles chemical analysis in that it breaks law down into fundamental constituent elements.[1] In any event, law proved to be his life's work. While employed as a law professor at Stanford, he submitted his first essay on 'Fundamental Legal Conceptions' to the *Yale Law Journal*. So deep was the impression made by the piece that Hohfeld was recruited to the Yale Law Faculty, and he remained at Yale until his premature death in October 1918. In four brief years at Yale 'Hohfeld generated an extraordinary intellectual excitement which carried over for a considerable period after his death'.[2]

Hohfeld was renowned as an exacting and uncompromising law teacher. He insisted on his students mastering the basic concepts of his analytical jurisprudence and employing them in their discussions of Equity and Conflict of Laws (these being the two courses which he taught). With many students he was unpopular, but he won the respect and admiration of the more able. After Hohfeld's death, a young Karl Llewellyn wrote a brief memoir of Hohfeld as a teacher, from a student viewpoint. While acknowledging that Hohfeld was a lonely figure who lacked the grace that makes for general popularity, Llewellyn found him to be an inspiring teacher. The following passage gives a flavour of Llewellyn's account:

> To have the vision lifted beyond the little point at hand, out of the single 'field' staked off as 'Bills and Notes' or 'Equity' - carried up into the high places, to look out over the whole land, hills and

> valleys, ploughed land and fallow, spread out in its wonder - this was the inspiration to be had in Hohfeld's classes.[3]

At his death, Hohfeld left behind him a fistful of law journal articles which apply his analysis to a variety of areas of legal doctrine; but the two essays on *Fundamental Legal Conceptions* (contained in the present volume) set out the basis of the analysis and form the intellectual centrepiece to Hohfeld's sadly curtailed life. Few works have made such a lasting contribution to analytical jurisprudence. The analysis of rights that Hohfeld offers is still regularly cited and relied upon by both lawyers and philosophers, and it is treated as a source of insight into the nature of moral rights as well as the legal rights that were Hohfeld's own focus of concern. Although some of his analytical distinctions were anticipated by earlier jurists, their insights were fragmentary and imperfect by comparison. Hohfeld's systematic and apparently exhaustive (yet concise) treatment is generally regarded as unsurpassed. This is not to say that he has not been criticised, but his book forms the essential starting point for any discussion of the nature and structure of rights.

At first glance, however, the book which lies before us is an unlikely contender for the title of jurisprudential 'classic', not so much because it is unfinished as because, on a superficial examination, it seems to belong to a genre of formalist legal scholarship that is now virtually extinct. Throughout the book, technical legal doctrines or institutions such as the trust, the *donatio mortis causa*, the escrow, and the sheriff's powers under a writ of execution are subjected to meticulous analysis in a manner calculated to mystify the student and irritate the practitioner. We have grown accustomed to a style of legal writing that is much more focused on practical questions of application than on the seemingly detached classificatory concerns that appear in Hohfeld. The reader in a hurry will conclude that Hohfeld's work presupposes a commitment to a formalist view of law as a body of highly systematic rules and doctrines yielding satisfactory answers in all cases, without the need to address questions of social policy. Within such a tradition, analysis and accurate taxonomy are intrinsically important, since they are thought to guarantee the central values of formal justice and predictability. For the modern reader, while a book which offered an intellectual defence of legal formalism might well rank as a jurisprudential classic, a book which embodies formalist assumptions in an uncritical and unreflective manner could not.

Yet, as we shall see, appearances can be misleading. Whether by accident or by design, Hohfeld's work, far from being a contribution to legal formalism, was one of the key intellectual developments which fundamentally shook established traditions of formalist scholarship.

In the opening pages of the work, Hohfeld raises the classic question of the nature of the trust. Does the beneficiary under a trust possess a right *in rem* (a proprietary right against the trust assets) or a mere right *in personam* against the trustee? It is not Hohfeld's immediate object to solve this puzzle. Rather he points out that a great diversity of solutions to it have been offered by lawyers from Coke to Maitland, and up to Hohfeld's own day, but it has been impossible for these lawyers to resolve the question satisfactorily because they have lacked 'a sufficiently comprehensive and discriminating analysis of jural relations in general.'[4] The same is true, he maintains, of a great many other legal problems. It is Hohfeld's intention to provide the basis for a solution by isolating and understanding 'the various fundamental conceptions that are involved in practically every legal problem'.[5]

Someone might object that inquiries of this type are without practical value. Not so, replies Hohfeld: questions such as that concerning the nature of the trust are of great significance, and a 'correct analysis of such interests would control the decision of a number of specific questions'.[6] Moreover, 'the deeper the analysis, the greater becomes one's perception of the unity and harmony in the law'.[7]

Remarks of this kind seems to rest upon an acceptance of formalism. The formalist regards law as a technical body of determinate rules, exhibiting a high degree of internal coherence, and holds that such rules can and should be applied without reference to open-ended questions of social policy. The anti-formalist, on the other hand, argues that rules should be applied in the light of the social policy that the rule is intended to serve. Some legal rules employ technical legal concepts such as 'offer for sale' or 'interest in land'. Because the formalist believes that reference to the particular policy served by a rule is unnecessary and undesirable, he will believe that a perfectly general definition of 'offer for sale' or 'interest in land' will be dispositive of questions about the applicability of those phrases for any rule in which they appear.[8] The anti-formalist will argue, on the other hand, that the wording of each rule must be interpreted in the context of the policies served by that rule; something may be an 'offer for sale' or an 'interest in land' for the purposes of one rule but not for the purposes of another; consequently the general analysis of such concepts, in detachment from questions about the applicability of particular rules, serves no useful purpose.

Hohfeld's belief that a general analysis of the nature of the trust (or a similarly general answer to some other taxonomic question) might control future decisions therefore seems to rest upon formalist assumptions.[9] Yet, even if this is so, it would be wrong to think of Hohfeld's own analytical contribution in *Fundamental Legal Conceptions* as resting upon formalism in a way that would rob the essay of interest for those who reject formalism. As we have seen, Hohfeld intended in *Fundamental Legal Conceptions* not to *resolve* questions such as those which would interest the formalist, but to provide the fundamental analysis which he saw as an essential *prerequisite* to the resolution of such questions. As we shall see, the analysis which he provided had the effect of exposing gaps in the path of formal reasoning that could only be filled by considerations of social policy or moral value. In this way, Hohfeld's work contributed to the decline of formalism itself. Whether or not he was himself a formalist, therefore, Hohfeld's analyses form a part of the series of intellectual developments that challenged and undermined formalism in the first half of the twentieth century.

Jural relations

Hohfeld tells us that it is an error to assume that all legal relations can be analysed in terms of rights and duties. The attempt so to analyse them leads to a 'chameleon-hued' use of the words 'right' and 'duty' whereby a single word is being employed to cover several distinct concepts. Hohfeld aims to isolate those distinct concepts, which he describes as 'the lowest common denominators of the law'.[10] Since the relevant concepts are fundamental and *sui generis*, Hohfeld treats them as not susceptible to formal definition. Instead, he sets them out in a scheme of 'opposites' and 'correlatives'. The scheme is as follows:

	(right	privilege	power	immunity
Jural Opposites	(			
	(no-right	duty	disability	liability
	(right	privilege	power	immunity
Jural Correlatives	(			
	(duty	no-right	liability	disability

To understand this scheme we must first understand that every jural relation is, for Hohfeld, a relationship between two persons.[11] The relationship is depicted most directly by the table of jural correlatives. Thus we may see from the table that, if X possesses a right, Y is under a duty; if X possesses a privilege, Y has a 'no-right'; if X possesses a power, Y is under a liability; and if X possesses an immunity, Y is under a disability. The table of jural opposites shows us that, for example, a privilege is the opposite of a duty; a power is the opposite of a disability; and so on. Rights, privileges, powers and immunities are all of them commonly referred to by lawyers as 'rights', but they are quite different in their implications and a more discriminating terminology would distinguish between them rigorously. It will serve the interests of clarity if we adopt a suggestion of Hohfeld's and refer to rights in the strict sense (i.e. 'right' as the correlative of 'duty') as 'claim-rights'.

Hohfeld supports his analysis of jural relations by detailed reference to cases. The gist of his argument is that, while judges frequently make mistakes as a result of the ambiguity of the word 'right' when it is used to cover claim-rights, privileges, powers and immunities, his analysis is nevertheless reflected in distinctions firmly embodied in the existing law. In summarising Hohfeld's analysis, we will for the most part omit discussion of the illustrative cases and doctrines which he cites.

Let us now consider each type of jural relation in turn.

The claim-right/duty relation

If I have a claim-right that you should pay me £5, it follows that you have a duty to pay me £5. If I have a claim-right that you should not assault me, you have a duty not to assault me. If I have a claim-right against you to be provided with work, then you are under a duty to provide me with work.

The privilege/no-right relation

Hohfeld chooses to use the term 'privilege' to refer to the absence of a duty. We will employ his usage here, but it is worth noting that many commentators prefer to substitute the term 'liberty'. A Hohfeldian privilege is in fact a liberty, in the sense of the absence of a duty. Thus, if I have a privilege to wear a hat, it follows that I am under no duty *not* to wear a hat. Since a privilege is a *jural* relation, not a factual one, it does not entail the absence of all obstruction or interference with my action, but merely the absence of a duty not to perform the action. I may have a privilege to wear a hat even if I have no hat to wear, and even if you have credibly threatened me with death should I wear a hat.

Since every jural relation holds between two persons, my privilege may exist as against some persons and not others. Thus, A may have a privilege to wear a hat as against B, but no such privilege as against C. This would be the case, for example, if A had made a contract with C under which A promised that he would not wear a hat. As against C, A would have a duty not to wear a hat (and C would have a correlative claim-right). As against B, A would retain his privilege to wear a hat, and B would have no right (i.e. a Hohfeldian 'no-right') that A should not wear a hat.

It is common for people to assume that, if A possesses a privilege to wear a hat, others are under a duty not to interfere with A's wearing of a hat; but within Hohfeld's analytical scheme this does not follow. No duties are entailed by the existence of a privilege. Duties are correlative not to privileges but to claim-rights. The contrary impression is a consequence of the existence of certain very general claim-rights/duties that have the effect of providing a perimeter of protection for Hohfeldian privileges.[12] For example, I have a duty not to assault you, and you have a claim-right that I should not assault you. Without assaulting you it may be difficult for me to interfere with your practice of wearing a hat. My duty not to assault you in that sense serves to protect your privilege to wear a hat; but it is not correlative to the privilege, and is logically separable from it. Thus one could imagine a game wherein I try to wear my hat and you try to prevent me from doing so. By consenting to play such a game I have exempted you from your duty not to carry out certain minor assaults upon me (such as knocking my hat off). I retain my privilege to wear a hat (since I am under no duty *not* to wear one) but you are under no duty not to prevent me from wearing a hat.

The power/liability relation

A person possesses power in Hohfeld's sense when they may, by their act, alter legal relations. Thus one may decide to transfer property to another, or enter into a contract, and in doing so one alters legal relations by assuming duties that one did not previously possess, negating existing duties, acquiring new powers, and so on. Like the other jural relations, the power/liability relation must be considered as obtaining between two persons. Thus X may have power as against Y but not as against Z. If, for example, Y makes X a contractual offer, X has the power by accepting the offer to place Y under certain contractual duties; but he has no such power as against Z, who made no offer.

Extreme confusion can be produced when lawyers refer to Hohfeldian powers as 'rights'. For example, a power may be combined with a duty not to exercise it, as when a non-owner has power to pass title in property but will be committing a tort in exercising the power. If we undiscriminatingly describe the power as a 'right', we will be forced to say that the non-owner has a right to sell the property, but will be committing a wrong in selling it. If we also describe Hohfeldian privileges as 'rights', we will be inclined to say, still more confusingly, that the non-owner has a right to sell (i.e. a power to sell) and has no right to sell (i.e. has no privilege to sell).

Power in X is correlative to 'liability' in Y. Hohfeld means by 'liability', the liability to have one's legal relations altered by the act of another. He points out that, just as lawyers have tended to refer to powers as 'rights', so they have tended to confuse this notion of 'liability' with the existence of a duty. Thus scholars have puzzled over the peculiar 'duties' incumbent upon those who exercise 'common callings' or operate public services, but Hohfeld points out that such puzzles arise from a failure to see that such persons are not under present duties but *liabilities*.

Correlative to those liabilities are the respective powers of the various members of the public. Thus, for example, a travelling member of the public has the legal power, by making proper application and sufficient tender, to impose a duty on the innkeeper to receive him as a guest.[13]

The immunity/disability relation

X possesses an immunity as against Y when Y has no power to change X's legal relations in a certain respect. For example, if Y has no power to place X under a duty to sing 'Rule Britannia', X has an immunity in that respect, and Y is under a disability. In some other respects, Y may have powers in relation to X. By making X a contractual offer, for example, Y confers upon X a power he would not otherwise possess: namely the power to conclude, if he so wishes, a contract with Y.

Constitutional Bills of Rights frequently confer extensive and very important immunities, in so far as, they disable the legislature from enacting certain types of law. A Bill of Rights guaranteeing 'freedom of speech', for example, may be understood as conferring an immunity against having certain duties restricting free speech imposed upon one by legislation. Such documents do not generally employ the Hohfeldian analytical apparatus, and it may therefore be far from clear whether a guaranteed 'right to free speech' is meant as a simple immunity, or whether the immunity might not be combined with certain claim-rights. Does the constitution impose a duty on government to take action restricting private interferences with free speech, for example? Similarly, an immunity may be combined with a power and with a claim-right. For example, a Bill of Rights may confer a right to vote in elections, and such a right may be analysed into a power to cast a valid vote, a claim-right against election officials requiring them to accept any such vote, and an immunity disabling the legislature from abridging such claim-rights and powers.

Multital relations and paucital relations

In his second essay, Hohfeld tackles the complex issue of the distinction between rights *in rem* and rights *in personam*. This is often regarded as a distinction between rights *over things* and rights *against persons*, but such an interpretation is clearly unacceptable. In the first place, it is obviously true that rights can only have juridical consequences for other persons, and can therefore only be rights against other persons, not *things*. Secondly, while civil law systems have commonly restricted the concept of 'property' to rights over physical things, the common law has never shared this restricted view.[14]

Having claimed in his first essay that the jural relations there identified are the fundamental elements in terms of which all legal institutions can be analysed, Hohfeld needed to demonstrate in his second essay that those same jural relations could be used to explicate the traditional distinction between rights *in rem* and *in personam*. He begins by suggesting that desirable substitutes for the terms '*in rem*' and '*in personam*' would be the terms 'multital' and 'paucital' respectively. Claim-rights, privileges, powers and immunities can each of them appear in both multital and paucital versions, giving us a total of eight categories.

The distinction between multital and paucital relations is best explained by means of an example. Suppose that I have a contract with you whereby you are obliged to manufacture a quantity of widgets. I have a claim-right against you and you have a correlative duty to manufacture the widgets. I might have a similar contract with another widget manufacturer, with similar consequences in terms of our claim-rights and duties. However many such contracts I have, however, my claim-rights are essentially limited to a definite number of persons. These are what Hohfeld calls 'paucital' claim-rights.

A paucital right, or claim (right *in personam*), is either a unique right residing in a person (or group of persons) and availing against a single person (or single group of persons); or else it is one of a few fundamentally similar, yet separate, rights availing respectively against a few definite persons.[15]

Suppose, on the other hand, that I am the owner of Blackacre. I have a claim-right that you should not enter the land without my consent. I have identical claim-rights against your mother, my employer, the Bishop of Ely, and anyone else that you care to mention. Each of these claim-rights is a consequence of[16] my ownership of Blackacre. There are 'multital-rights'.

A multital right, or claim (right *in rem*), is always *one* of a large class of *fundamentally similar* yet separate rights, actual and potential, residing in a *single* person (or single group of persons) but availing *respectively* against persons constituting a very large and indefinite class of people.[17]

This analysis enables Hohfeld to explain the distinction between rights *in rem* and *in personam* in terms of his basic analysis of jural relations. It also enables him to argue that, not only is a right *in rem* (or multital right) not a right *against a thing*, it is not always a right *relating to a thing*. Thus, my claim-right that you should not assault me is a multital right, since it is only one member of a large class of similar rights holding against an indefinite number of people (i.e. I have a right that your mother should not assault me, a right that the Bishop of Ely should not assault me, and so on). If one objected that the claim-right not to be assaulted is a right in relation to a thing in so far as it concerns the integrity of my body, Hohfeld would offer a different example: 'a patentee's right, or claim, that any ordinary person shall not manufacture articles covered by the patent.'[18]

On a Hohfeldian analysis, the owner of Blackacre possesses not a single right over an area of land, but a complex aggregation of claim-rights, powers, privileges and immunities. For example, the owner has a series of multital claim-rights that persons should not trespass on the land; a series of multital privileges to enter upon and exploit the land himself; a series of multital powers to transfer title to the land or create lesser interests in it, such as leases or easements; and a series of multital immunities against having his title affected by the acts of other persons.[19]

Hohfeld's lesson for formalism

The demonstration that property rights can be broken down into complex bundles of claim-rights, powers, privileges and immunities was to have a dramatic impact upon legal thinking. In the first place, it demonstrated that no firm juridical consequences can be inferred from the general proposition that someone enjoys a 'property right' in, or is the 'owner' of, a certain resource. Such general claims have little real content until they are fleshed out in terms of Hohfeldian jural relations. Yet general claims of precisely that type tended to form key steps in the reasoning of formalist judges. By revealing complex multiplicity beneath the surface of apparently unitary concepts, Hohfeld had helped to undermine the claim of legal doctrine to form a tightly deductive and self-contained body of reasoning.[20]

Moreover, his analysis made it abundantly clear that the property owner's rights were not conferred solely to protect the owner's own use of the resource in question, but had much a wider significance:

It is sometimes thought that A's rights, or claims, are created by the law for the sole purpose of guarding or protecting A's own physical use or enjoyment of the land, as if such physical use or enjoyment of the land were the only economic factor of importance. A moment's reflection, however, shows that this is a very inadequate view. Even though the land be entirely vacant and A have no intention whatever of personally using the land, his rights or claims that others shall not use it even temporarily in such ways as would not alter its physical character are, generally, of great economic significance as tending to make others compensate A in exchange for the extinguishment of his rights, or claims, or in other words, the creation of privileges of use and enjoyment.[21]

In this way, Hohfeld's work contributed to a tradition of thought that portrayed ownership as a power of command over persons, analogous to the power of the state, and that contested the claim of the market to be a form of distribution free from coercion.[22] The Hohfeldian disaggregation of property rights has also been invoked in support of models of market socialism, in order to resist the suggestion that full private ownership and full state ownership are the only genuine alternatives.[23]

It was not solely in his treatment of property rights, however, that Hohfeld's analysis eroded the seeming plausibility of formalism. Although Hohfeld sought to demonstrate that his fundamental jural relations were recognised and embodied in existing judicial decisions, many of his illustrative discussions exposed serious equivocations in the opinions of judges and legal writers. By employing the single word 'right' to cover distinct legal conceptions, judgments sometimes gave the appearance of having a logically deductive structure, whereas that appearance could be dissolved by imposing the discipline of the Hohfeldian categories.

A good example is provided by Hohfeld's discussion of Lord Lindley's judgment in *Quinn* v *Leathem*.[24] Quinn tried to force Leathem, a butcher, to sack his non-union employees and employ only union members. In pursuit of this objective, Quinn threatened a strike at the shop of one of Leathem's customers unless the customer would stop doing business with Leathem. Leathem sued Quinn. In a passage quoted by Hohfeld, Lord Lindley set out a line of reasoning that may be represented thus:

(i) Leathem was at liberty to earn his living in his own way;
(ii) this liberty included the liberty to deal with other persons who were willing to deal with him;
(iii) therefore, everyone was under a duty not to prevent the exercise of that liberty;
(iv) Quinn had violated that duty.

At first glance this reasoning appears to move deductively from a wholly uncontroversial proposition of law at (i) to a conclusion at (iv). Once we apply the Hohfeldian analysis, however, we can see that the moves are not purely deductive. Proposition (i) is wholly uncontroversial only if Leathem's 'liberty' is taken to be a Hohfeldian privilege. It is indeed uncontroversial that Leathem was under no duty not to earn his living in his own way (that being all that is involved in a privilege). But no conclusions about the duties of other persons are entailed by the existence of a privilege. Such conclusions could legitimately be drawn (i.e. the step taken at (iii)) only if Leathem's 'liberty' was in fact a claim-right not to be interfered with. We could, therefore, render the argument deductive if we construed step (i), in an appropriate way, as involving a claim-right. While that might make the argument deductive, however, it would also rob it of its uncontroversial basic premise. If step (i) involved the assertion of a claim-right for Leathem, it would not be uncontroversial, since the existence or non-existence of such a claim-right is the whole issue in dispute between the parties.

This is not to say that Lord Lindley was muddled. What he needed to decide was whether Leathem's acknowledged 'liberty' (or Hohfeldian 'privilege') should be protected by a claim-right against conduct of the kind that Quinn had engaged in. That is, in effect, what his judgment decides. But the decision does not flow smoothly and inevitably from established legal entitlements. Rather, the step from finding a Hohfeldian privilege to protecting it with a Hohfeldian claim-right involves a judgement of social policy or moral principle: one has to address the question of whether Leathem's privilege *ought* to be so protected.

The use of the term 'right' to cover both privileges and claim-rights is a particularly useful way for formalist judges to conceal (perhaps even from themselves) the moral or social policy judgements underpinning their decisions. Whenever one is not under a duty to perform a certain act, one has a privilege to perform it; by describing that privilege as a 'right', a judge can move illegitimately to the conclusion that others are under a duty not to interfere. In this way, new duties can be imposed without any acknowledgment that the law has been changed.

Correlativity

Hohfeld is usually regarded as offering an analysis of rights. Yet he himself claims to be offering an analysis of the fundamental elements of *all* jural relations. Judged in the light of this claim, Hohfeld's analysis is problematic in so far as it holds that every legal duty is correlative to a claim-right in some other person. Many jurists would contend that this is not so. Some legal duties, they would argue, are correlative to legal rights while others are not. In particular, duties in private law *are* generally correlative to rights, while duties imposed in criminal law, or regulatory public laws such as tax laws, are not correlative to rights.

This debate is in fact connected with a deeper one, which Hohfeld does not address: the dispute between the 'interest' and 'will' theories of rights. Hohfeld tells us that a duty is correlative to a claim-right and *vice versa*; but what exactly is the relationship of correlativity involved here? If we are provided with information about the content of someone's duty (e.g. I am under a duty to whistle 'Rule Britannia' every third Sunday in the month) what additional information would we need in order to identify the correlative claim-right (if there is such a right)? Until we can answer this question we have no way of deciding whether claim-rights are or are not always correlative to duties.

Crudely summarising a complex debate, we may say that the 'will theory' claims that X possesses a claim-right when the enforcement of Y's duty is dependent upon an exercise of will by X. Thus, private law duties are correlative to rights because they are enforced only at the instance of private parties. The 'interest theory', on the other hand, claims that a duty in Y is correlative to a claim-right in X when Y's duty was imposed by the law in order to protect X's interest. On this view, even the duties of criminal law may be correlative to claim-rights, since those duties are (arguably) imposed in order to protect the interests of individuals, even though those individuals do not possess the power to control enforcement of the duties.

Although some prominent legal positivists have been and are advocates of the interest theory, there is a sense in which the will theory sits better with the strict separation of law and morality insisted upon by positivism. Equally, the will theory seems more consistent with a legal formalist approach that resists attempts to collapse the interpretation of legal rules back into questions about the social policies served by the rules. For, according to the interest-theory, one needs to make a judgement about the policies served by a legal duty (i.e. about the interests it was intended to protect) before one can identify the right to which it is correlative. On the will-theory, by contrast, such rights might be identifiable simply by reference to the formal structures of the law (e.g. does enforcement depend upon a private exercise of will?) without any need to raise questions about the policies served by the rules.[25]

Recently, the will theory has fallen out of fashion. Contemporary defenders of the interest theory, however, do not assert a universal correlativity of rights and duties. In fact, they deny correlativity altogether. Thus, Neil MacCormick has argued that a right is not the strict correlative of a duty, logically entailed by the duty, but a reason for imposing a duty or some other form of legal protection.[26] In saying that X has a right to a certain level of income, for example, we are saying that X's interest in receiving that level of income is so important that it ought to be protected. We might protect it by placing a duty on X's employer to pay a minimum wage; or a duty on the state to provide welfare benefits. Conceivably, the right might be protected by giving X certain immunities and imposing disabilities on others: e.g. one could impose on state authorities a disability to make cuts in welfare provision for X, or by granting X an immunity against being dismissed by his employer.[27]

MacCormick's version of the interest theory makes rights discoverable only by an inquiry into the justificatory basis of the law in social policy or moral value. Hohfeldian claim-rights, powers, privileges and immunities are on this view merely the instrumental mechanisms whereby deeper rights are protected. In some respects this is an attractive analysis, since it suggests a way in which the law may be thought of as an organic system with a an integrity of its own. The conferment of a Hohfeldian claim-right, power, privilege or immunity might be regarded as the *recognition* of a deeper right (i.e. an important human interest meriting protection). On this view, there might at any one time be recognised legal rights which lack adequate protection; and such rights would be legal reasons for creating new claim-rights, powers, privileges or immunities. In this analysis, the law is not a long list of duties which is added to whenever social policy considerations make that appropriate; new duties (or disabilities, privileges, etc.) may be added on the basis of specifically legal considerations in the attempt to give better legal recognition to established legal rights.

In a sense, MacCormick's analysis is not inconsistent with Hohfeld's, but operates at a different level. Hohfeld offers us a refined set of tools for reporting the precise content of settled legal rules at the cutting edge of immediately available remedies. MacCormick, on the other hand, offers an interpretation of the structures of doctrinal reasoning leading to the establishment of such rules, and suggesting the desirability of providing new remedies.

More radical critics might here object that the very notion of 'settled legal rules' is misconceived. For example, Arthur Jacobson has argued that Hohfeld's system misrepresents the character of the common law precisely because the common law is not a system of determinate rules:

> [R]eports of cases, not black-letter rules, are the first place to look for rights and obligations. Though cases often state rules (often they do not) , the rules per se are never the law, only a way of talking about its formulation ... So purveyors of black-letter compilations and lawyers who confine their practice to these compilations without studying cases are traitors to Common Law.[28]

The dynamic character of the common law, firmly rooted in the details of case-law and incapable of accurate depiction in the form of a set of rules, renders Hohfeld's analysis inapplicable in Jacobson's view. A judgment never establishes, for example, that someone has a 'privilege' to act in a certain way or that others have 'no-right' that they should not so act. If my legal action against you is unsuccessful, all that the resulting judgment establishes is that I have not so far succeeded in establishing the existence of a right against you. I may devise a new argument which succeeds in establishing a right against you. It is true that the doctrine of *res judicata* may prevent me from bringing a further action, but (Jacobson points out) such a doctrine is not a logically necessary feature of legal systems. It follows, he argues, that my present 'no-right' does not entail your 'privilege'.[29]

The essential modernity of Hohfeld

Jacobson presents his argument as a challenge to *correlativity*, but this may not be the most fruitful way to consider the substantive points which he makes; perhaps he is better thought of as challenging the very idea of a static representation of the existing law, rather than as rejecting one specific feature (correlativity) of such representation. The suggestion that there is a deep incompatibility between Hohfeld's analysis and the nature of the common law merits further consideration, however. For it is true that the common law was originally a body of remedies, not a system of rights. Only with the rise of systematic treatises on law, in the late eighteenth and nineteenth centuries, was there a serious attempt to expound the common law as a body of substantive principles conferring rights. Fitting the common law with a systematic framework constructed in terms of rights was no easy matter.[30] Many of the judges who are taken to task by Hohfeld for their conceptual errors are in fact wrestling with this long standing problem. This raises the possibility that the problem is insoluble, and that the fluid and open-ended character of the common law cannot without distortion be translated into a static system of rights, powers, privileges and immunities.[31] Perhaps Hohfeld is a late contributor to a tradition of legal scholarship that sought to *Romanise* the common law by translating it into a language of rights and duties, thereby making its representation in static textbook form a possibility.

If Hohfeld's analysis fails to fit the character of the historic common law, however, it may nevertheless point the way to the future. The traditional common law depended upon the existence of a small and relatively stable society where shared understandings could easily be preserved amongst a narrow cadre of judges and lawyers.[32] The rise of the systematic legal treatise, and the attempt to systematise legal doctrine in terms of rights, was in part a response to the pressures upon this stable common law ethos. Yet the very pressures that accentuated the need for systematic expositions of legal doctrine also undercut their possibility. With the rise of a regulatory state that employed law to grapple with a host of problems and to pursue infinitely diverse social policies, legal doctrine could no longer be represented as founded on any coherent set of doctrinal principles serving to unify and stabilise the multiplicity of black-letter rules.[33] The exposition of legal doctrine has increasingly become a matter of setting out detailed rules at a low level of abstraction, often in the light of a variety of *ad hoc* social policies that those rules are thought to advance and in the light of which they should be interpreted. There is little or no expectation that these multifarious policies will form any coherent or systematically intelligible structure.

We noted earlier that Hohfeld's concept of 'privilege' is a common source of confusion, since people tend to assume that a 'privilege' or liberty to perform an act entails that others are under a duty not to interfere with that performance. In Hohfeld's system, no such duty is entailed. On the popular view, by contrast, claim-rights and privileges are inextricably linked: if one has a 'right' to perform an act, the act is both permissible and inviolable. It is permissible in so far as there is no duty not to perform the act; and it is inviolable in so far as there is a duty on others not to interfere with the act. Hohfeld separates the two facets of the right in order to construct his two concepts of 'claim-right' and 'privilege'.

Why should we prefer Hohfeld's analysis to the popular view that rights entail both permissibility and inviolability? The answer that I wish to suggest is as follows. When the law pursues some scheme of mutually compatible liberties, the choice between Hohfeldian and popular views may make little difference: indeed there may be much to recommend the popular view. But when the law seeks to protect or advance large numbers of *mutually competing* interests or liberties, the position is changed. When the law serves mutually competing interests, use of the popular concept of a right would generate contradictions. The Hohfeldian analysis is necessary to avoid those contradictions. The Hohfeldian analysis is therefore the most appropriate analysis of rights for a regulatory welfare state that employs law to implement a great diversity of mutually competitive social policies.

On the popular view, a right to perform an action renders the action both permissible and inviolable. Hillel Steiner has demonstrated that, on this understanding of rights, rights could not conflict without generating logical contradictions. Suppose that X has a right to perform action A and Y has a right to perform action B. Suppose also that Y's performance of B would interfere with X's performance of A. It follows that B is both *permissible* (as being an exercise of Y's right) and *impermissible* (as being a violation of X's right). Steiner goes on to argue that a system of rights which is to avoid this type of contradiction would have to take the form of a system of entitlements to the exclusive use of objects and spaces.[34] A body of laws of the modern regulatory type, would inevitably generate numerous conflicts between rights. The application to such a system of the popular concept of a right (combining permissibility and inviolability) would generate contradiction. It would seem to follow that the Hohfeldian analysis of rights (separating permissibility and inviolability as the characteristics of privileges and claim-rights respectively) is the most appropriate one for a modern system of law.

Somewhat similar observations apply to Hohfeld's analysis of 'multital' and 'paucital' rights. As we have seen, Steiner argues that a system of rights (in the traditional sense of 'right' that combines permissibility and inviolability) that is free from contradiction would have to take the form of entitlements to the exclusive use of objects and spaces. The argument helps us to grasp the special moral importance of such entitlements in a scheme of rights based upon the value of liberty.[35] Hohfeld's analysis, however, by breaking the connection between conceptions of property and control over physical things and spaces, suppresses that distinct moral importance. Here too, Hohfeld's analysis reflects the values of the regulatory welfare state.

Is it also possible to relate the differences between Hohfeld and MacCormick to the rise of the regulatory state and the erosion of traditional legal values? As we have already explained, MacCormick's view of rights suggests that law is not a long list of duties which is added to whenever social policy considerations make that appropriate; new duties (or disabilities, privileges, etc.) may be added on the basis of specifically legal considerations in the attempt to give better legal recognition to established legal rights. While Hohfeld's analysis might be an adequate basis for the static representation of settled legal rules, it fails (by its insistence on strict correlativity) to exhibit the deeper level of doctrinal coherence in the law, whereby rights as fundamental interests are recognised and may receive protection through a variety of legal devices (such as Hohfeldian claim-rights, powers, privileges and immunities).

If, however, there is any truth in the suggestion that deep doctrinal coherence is absent from modern regulatory systems of law, static representation of settled rules may be the best that we can hope for. No doubt a range of human interests can be listed and will be found to underpin many legal provisions. These interests can, for what it is worth, be labelled 'rights'. But conflict between these interests will be so pervasive, and the nature of their reconciliation so much a matter of social policy judgement rather than doctrinal reasoning, that the language of rights will here preserve the empty facade of doctrinal integrity without its substance. In such circumstances, a Hohfeldian approach which, simply and without further pretension, reports the instrumentalities by which interests are protected may be the more honest approach.

Hohfeld may himself have entertained some of the characteristic beliefs of formalism, such as the conviction that a purely technical analysis of legal concepts might reveal 'fundamental unity and harmony in the law'.[36] Yet his analysis exposed the vulnerability of such formalist views. Formalism was itself an attempt to preserve ideas of deep doctrinal coherence in a changing world where coherence was undercut by the massive expansion of legal regulation. Perhaps contrary to his own hopes and intentions, Hohfeld may have provided us with an apparatus of concepts well suited to the character of the modern law. At the beginning of the twenty-first century, the importance of his analysis remains undiminished.[37]

Notes

1 W Twining, *Karl Llewellyn and the Realist Movement* (1973) 36-37.
2 *Ibid* 34.
3 Llewellyn, 'Wesley Newcomb Hohfeld: Teacher' (1918) 28 *Yale Law Journal* 795, 796.
4 22 below.
5 *Ibid.*
6 21 below.
7 48 below.

8 A good example of such formalism is provided by *Fisher* v *Bell* [1961] 1 QB 394.

9 Some caution is warranted here, since Hohfeld occasionally cites anti-formalist pronouncements with approval. Thus, near the start of his second essay, he quotes Mr Justice Holmes' criticisms of the tendency to be led 'by a technical definition to apply a certain name, and then to deduce consequences which have no relation to the grounds on which the name was applied'. n 141 below. However, many lawyers might agree with Holmes' observation whilst failing to see that such strictures could justly be applied to a great many of the intellectual operations of traditional formalist scholarship.

10 48 below.

11 Here Hohfeld draws on a well established tradition of thought. Eg FK von Savigny, *Jural Relations* (translation by WH Rattigan of *System of Modern Roman Law*, vol 2) (1978) s 60: 'every jural relation consists in the relation of one person to another person'.

12 HLA Hart, *Essays on Bentham* (1982) 166-173.

13 43 below.

14 For a useful discussion see Kahn-Freund's introduction to K Renner, *The Institutions of Private Law and Their Social Functions* (1949) 20. See also NE Simmonds, *The Decline of Juridical Reason* (1984) 122-127.

15 53 below.

16 More accurately, it is one of the constituents of my ownership.

17 53 below.

18 64 below. See also J Waldron, *The Right to Private Property* (1988) 33-37 and S Munzer, *A Theory of Property* (1990) 72-74.

19 For a helpful analysis see Honore, 'Ownership' in AG Guest, ed, *Oxford Essays in Jurisprudence* (1961).

20 Hohfeld's analysis also poses severe problems for the 'takings' doctrine developed under the US Fifth Amendment. The Fifth Amendment provides that 'private property' shall not be taken for public use without just compensation. But what is property? On one view, 'property' might include all the multital rights that we enjoy, but such an interpretation would operate to hamstring modern government. See B Ackerman, *Private Property and the Constitution* (1977) and R Epstein, *Takings: Private Property and the Power of Eminent Domain* (1985).

21 76 below.

22 See Cohen, 'Property and Sovereignty' (1927) 13 *Cornell Law Quarterly* 8; Hale 'Bargaining, Duress and Economic Liberty' (1943) 43 *Columbia Law Review* 603 and JR Commons, *Legal Foundations of Capitalism* (1924). See also H Kelsen, *Introduction to the Problems of Legal Theory* (1992) 41-42.

23 See D Miller, *Market, State and Community* (1989) 53.

24 [1901] AC 495. Hohfeld's discussion is at 34-35 below.

25 See H Kelsen, *Introduction to the Problems of Legal Theory* (1992) 44.

26 See MacCormick 'Rights in Legislation' in PMS Hacker and J Raz, *Law, Morality and Society* (1977). MacCormick is concerned to attack the will-theory rather than Hohfeld. But his attack is relevant to Hohfeld in so far as it focusses upon the issue of correlativity. See also J Raz, 'Legal Rights' (1984) 4 *Oxford Journal of Legal Studies* 1.

27 For criticism of this position see NE Simmonds, *Central Issues in Jurisprudence* (1986) 133-139.

28 Jacobson, 'Hegel's Legal Plenum', in D Cornell, M Rosenfeld and D Gray Carlson, eds, *Hegel and Legal Theory* (1991) 106. Cf K Llewellyn, *The Bramble Bush* (1960) 96-97.

29 Jacobson, 'Hegel's Legal Plenum' 101-102.

30 See Simmonds, 'Reason, History and Privilege: Blackstone's Debt to Natural Law' (1988) 105 *Zeitschrift der Savigny-Stiftung fur Rechtsgeschichte: Germanistische Abteilung* 200.

31 Cf Fried, 'Rights and the Common Law', in RG Frey, ed, *Utility and Rights* (1985). See also the following observation from Milsom: 'I have an uncomfortable theory that once any body of law can be written out in a text-book it is incapable of a true response'. SFC Milsom, *Studies in the History of the Common Law* (1985) 212.

32 See Simpson, 'The Common Law and Legal Theory', in AWB Simpson, ed, *Oxford Essays in Jurisprudence (Second Series)* (1973).

33 See NE Simmonds, The Decline of Juridical Reason (1984).

34 Steiner, 'The Structure of a Set of Compossible Rights' (1977) 74 *Journal of Philosophy* 767.

35 See also Steiner, 'Individual Liberty' (1974-75) 75 *Proceedings of the Aristotelian Society* 33.

36 48 below.

37 Hohfeld's analysis and its significance are discussed at length in MH Kramer, NE Simmonds and H Steiner, *A Debate Over Rights* (1998).

Bibliography

Hohfeld's publications

'The Nature of Stockholders' Individual Liability for Corporation Debts' (1909) 9 *Columbia Law Review* 285.

'The Individual Liability of Stockholders and the Conflict of Laws' (1909) 9 *Columbia Law Review* 492; (1910) 10 *Columbia Law Review* 283; (1910) 10 *Columbia Law Review* 520.

'The Relations Between Equity and Law' (1913) 11 *Michigan Law Review* 537.

'Some Fundamental Legal Conceptions as Applied in Judicial Reasoning' (1913) 23 *Yale Law Journal* 16; (1917) 26 *Yale Law Journal* 710.

'The Need of Remedial Legislation in the California Law of Trusts and Perpetuities' (1913) 1 *California Law Review* 305.
'A Vital School of Jurisprudence and Law' [1914] *Proceedings of Association of American Law Schools for 1914* 76.
'Supplemental Note on the Conflict of Equity and Law' (1917) 26 *Yale Law Journal* 767.
'Faulty Analysis in Easement and License Cases' (1917) 27 *Yale Law Journal* 66.

Note: All these publications were reproduced in the enlarged 1923 edition of *Fundamental Legal Conceptions, As Applied in Judicial Reasoning: And Other Legal Essays* (see Preface to this edition).

Some other relevant books and essays

W W Cook 'Hohfeld's Contributions to the Science of Law' (1919) 28 *Yale Law Journal* 721 (also in W N Hohfeld, *Fundamental Legal Conceptions* (1919)).
A L Corbin, 'Foreword', in W N Hohfeld, *Fundamental Legal Conceptions* (1964).
A L Corbin, 'Jural Relations and their Classification' (1921) 30 *Yale Law Journal* 226.
G Marshall 'Rights, Options and Entitlements', in A W B Simpson, ed, *Oxford Essays in Jurisprudence* (Second Series) (1973).
M Radin, 'A Restatement of Hohfeld' (1938) 51 *Harvard Law Review* 1141.
J Singer 'The Legal Rights Debate in Analytical Jurisprudence from Bentham to Hohfeld' [1982] *Wisconsin Law Review* 975.
H Steiner, *An Essay on Rights* (1994).
L W Sumner, *The Moral Foundation of Rights* (1987).
J J Thomson, *The Realm of Rights* (1990).
C Wellman, *A Theory of Rights* (1985).
A White, *Rights* (1984).
G Williams 'The Concept of Legal Liberty' (1956) 56 *Columbia Law Review* 1129 (also in R Summers, ed, *Essays in Legal Philosophy* (1968)).

FUNDAMENTAL LEGAL CONCEPTIONS

Section 1

From very early days down to the present time the essential nature of trusts and other equitable interests has formed a favourite subject for analysis and disputation. The classical discussions of Bacon[1] and Coke are familiar to all students of equity, and the famous definition of the great chief justice (however inadequate it may really be) is quoted even in the latest text-books on trusts.[2] That the subject has had a peculiar fascination for modern legal thinkers is abundantly evidenced by the well-known articles of Langdell[3] and Ames,[4] by the oft-repeated observation of Maitland in his *Lectures on Equity*,[5] by the very divergent treatment of Austin in his *Lectures on Jurisprudence*,[6] by the still bolder thesis of Salmond in his volume on *Jurisprudence*,[7] and by the discordant utterances of Mr Hart[8] and Mr Whitlock[9] in their very recent contribution to our periodical literature.

It is believed that all of the discussions and analyses referred to are inadequate. Perhaps, however, it would have to be admitted that even the great intrinsic interest of the subject itself and the note-worthy divergence of opinion existing among thoughtful lawyers of all times would fail to afford more than a comparatively slight excuse for any further discussion considered as a mere end in itself. But, quite apart from the presumably practical consideration of endeavouring to 'think straight' in relation to all legal problems, it is apparent that the true analysis of trusts and other equitable interests is a matter that should appeal to even the most extreme pragmatists of the law. It may well be that one's view as to the correct analysis of such interests would control the decision of a number of specific questions. This is obviously true as regards the solution of many difficult and delicate problems in constitutional law and in the conflict of laws.[10] So, too, in certain questions in the law of perpetuities, the intrinsic nature of equitable interests is of great significance, as attested by the well-known *Gomm* case[11] and others more or less similar. The same thing is apt to be true of a number of special questions relating to the subject of *bona fide* purchase for value. So on indefinitely.[12]

But all this may seem like misplaced emphasis; for the suggestions last made are not peculiarly applicable to equitable interests: the same points and the same examples seem valid in relation to all possible kinds of jural interests, legal as well as equitable, - and that too, whether we are concerned with 'property,' 'contracts,' 'torts,' or any other title of the law. Special reference has therefore been made to the subject of trusts and other equitable interests only for the reason that the striking divergence of opinion relating thereto conspicuously exemplifies the need for dealing somewhat more intensively and systematically than is usual with the nature and analysis of all types of jural interests. Indeed, it would be virtually impossible to consider the subject of trusts at all adequately without, at the very threshold, analyzing and discriminating the various fundamental conceptions that are involved in practically every legal problem. In this connection the suggestion may be ventured that the usual discussions of trusts and the other jural interests seem inadequate (and at times misleading) for the very reason that they are not founded on a sufficiently comprehensive and discriminating analysis of jural relations in general. Putting the matter in another way, the tendency - and the fallacy - has been to treat the specific problem as if it were far less complex and it really is; and this commendable effort to treat as simple that which is really complex has, it is believed, furnished a serious obstacle to the clear understanding, the orderly statement, and the correct solution of legal problems. In short, it is submitted that the right kind of simplicity can result only from more searching and more discriminating analysis.

If, therefore, the title of this article suggests a merely philosophical inquiry as to the nature of law and legal relations, - a discussion regarded more or less as an end in itself, - the writer may be pardoned for repudiating such a connotation in advance. On the contrary, in response to the invitation of the editor of this journal, the main purpose of the writer is to emphasize certain oft-neglected matters that may aid in the understanding and in the solution of practical, everyday problems of the law. With this end in view, the present article and another soon to follow will discuss, as of chief concern, the basic conceptions of the law, - the legal elements that enter into all types of jural interests. A later article will deal specially with the analysis of certain typical and important interests of a complex character, - more particularly trusts and other equitable interests. In passing, it seems necessary to state that both of these articles are intended more for law school students than for any other class of readers. For that reason, it is hoped that the more learned reader may pardon certain parts of the discussion that might otherwise seem unnecessarily elementary and detailed. On the other hand, the limits of space inherent in a periodical article must furnish the excuse for as great a brevity of treatment as is consistent with clearness, and for a comparatively meager discussion - or which might otherwise merit greater attention. In short, the emphasis is to be placed on those points believed to have the greatest practical value.

Legal Conceptions Contrasted with Non-Legal Conceptions

At the very outset it seems necessary to emphasize the importance of differentiating purely legal relations from the physical and mental facts that call such relations into being. Obvious as this initial suggestion may seem to be, the arguments that one may hear in court almost any day, and likewise a considerable number of judicial opinions, afford ample evidence of the inveterate and unfortunate tendency to confuse and blend the legal and the non-legal quantities in a given problem. There are at least two special reasons for this.

For one thing, the association of ideas involved in the two sets of relations - the physical and the mental on the one hand, and the purely legal on the other - is, in the very nature of the case. Extremely close. This fact has necessarily had a marked influence upon the general doctrines and the specific rules of early systems of law. Thus, we are told by Pollock and Maitland:

> Ancient German law, like ancient roman law, sees great difficulties in the way of an assignment of a debt or other benefit of a contract ... men do not see how there can be a transfer of a right unless that right is embodied in some corporeal thing.[13] The history of the incorporeal things has shown us this; they are not completely transferred until the transferee has obtained seisin, has turned his beasts onto the pasture, presented a clerk to the church or hanged a thief upon the gallows. A covenant or a warranty of title may be so bound up with land that the assignee of the land will be able to sue the covenantor or warrantor.[14]

In another connection, the same learned authors observe:

> The realm of mediaeval law is rich with incorporeal things. Any permanent right which is of a transferable nature, at al events if it has what we may call a territorial ambit, is thought of as a thing that is very like a piece of land. Just because it is a thing it is transferable. This is no fiction invented by the speculative jurists. For the popular mind these things are things. The lawyer's business is not to make them things but to point out that they are incorporeal. The layman

> who wishes to convey the advowson of a church will say that what he means to transfer is not that structure of wood and stone which belongs to God and the saints, but a thing incorporeal, as incorporeal as how own soul or the *anima mundi.*[15]

A second reason for the tendency to confuse or blend non-legal and legal conceptions consist in the ambiguity and looseness of our legal terminology. The word 'property' furnishes a striking example. Both with lawyers and with laymen this term has no definite or stable connotation. Sometimes it is employed to indicate the physical object to which various legal rights, privileges, etc., relate; then again - with far greater discrimination and accuracy - the word is used to denote the legal interest (or aggregate of legal relations) appertaining to such physical object. Frequently there is a rapid and fallacious shift from the one meaning to the other. At times, also, the term is used in such a 'blended' sense as to convey no definite meaning whatever.

For the purpose of exemplifying the looser usage just referred to, we may quote from *Wilson* v *Ward Lumber Co*:

> The term 'property,' as commonly used, denotes any external object over which the right of property is exercised. In this sense it is a very wide term, and includes every class of acquisitions which a man can own or have an interest in.[16]

Perhaps the ablest statement to exemplify the opposite and more accurate usage is that of Professor Jeremiah Smith (then Mr Justice Smith) in the leading case of *Eaton* v *B C and M R R Co*:

> In a strict legal sense, land is not 'property,' but the subject of property. The term 'property,' although in common parlance frequently applied to a tract of land or a chattel, in its legal significance 'means only the rights of the owner in relation to it.' 'It denotes a right over a determinate thing.' 'Property is the right of any person to possess, use, enjoy, and dispose of a thing.' (Selden, J., in *Wynehamer* v *People*, 13 N.Y., 378, p.433; 1 Blackstone's Com., 138; 2 Austin's *Jurisprudence*, 3d ed., 817, 818) ... The right of indefinite user (or of using indefinitely) is an essential quality of absolute property, without which absolute property can have no existence ... This right of user necessarily includes the right and power of excluding others from using the land. (See 2 *Austin on*

> *Jurisprudence*, 3d ed., 836; Wells, J., in *Walker* v *O.C.W.R.R.*, 103 Mass., 10, p.14).[17]

Another useful passage is to be found in the opinion of Sherwood J in *St Louis* v *Hall*:

> Sometimes the term is applied to the thing itself, as a horse, or a tract of land; these things, however, though the subjects of property, are, when coupled with possession, but the *indicia*, the visible manifestation of invisible rights, the evidence of things not seen ... Property, then, in a determinate object, is composed of certain constituent elements. To wit: the unrestricted right of use, enjoyment, and disposal, of that object.[18]

In connection with the ambiguities latent in the term 'property' it seems well to observe that similar looseness of thought and expression lurks in the supposed (but false) contrast between 'corporeal' and 'incorporeal' property. The second passage above quoted from Pollock and Maitland exhibits one phase of this matter. For further striking illustration, reference may be made to Blackstone's well-known discussion of corporeal and incorporeal heraditaments. Thus, the great commentator tells us:

> But an hereditament [says Sir Edward Coke] is by much the largest and most comprehensive expression; for it includes not only lands and tenements, but, whatsoever *may be inherited*, be it corporeal or incorporeal, real, personal, or mixed.[19]

It is clear that only *legal interests* as such can be inherited; yet in the foregoing quotation there is an inextricable confusion between the physical or 'corporeal' objects and the corresponding legal interests, all of which latter must necessarily be 'incorporeal' or 'invisible,' to use the expression of Mr Justice Sherwood. This ambiguity of thought and language continues throughout Blackstone's discussion; for a little later he says:

> Hereditaments, then, to use the largest expression, are of two kinds, corporeal and incorporeal. Corporeal consist of such as affect the senses, such as may be seen and handled by the body; incorporeal are not the objects of sensation, can neither be seen nor handled; are creatures of the mind, and exist only in contemplation.

Still further on he says:

> An incorporeal heraditament is a right issuing out of a thing corporate (whether real or personal), or concerning, or annexed to, or exercisable within, the same ... Incorporeal heraditaments are principally of ten sorts: advowsons, tithes, commons, ways, offices, dignities, franchises, corodies or pensions, annuities, and rents.

Since all legal interests are 'incorporeal' - consisting, as they do, of more or less limited aggregates of *abstract* legal relations - such a supposed contrast as that sought to be drawn by Blackstone can but serve to mislead the unwary. The legal interest of the fee simple owner of land and the comparatively limited interest of the owner of a 'right of way' over such land are alike so far as 'incorporeality' is concerned; the true contrast consists, of course, primarily in the fact that the fee simple owner's aggregate of legal relations is far more extensive than the aggregate of the easement owner.
Much of the difficulty, as regards legal terminology, arises from the fact that many of our words were originally applicable only to physical things;[20] so that their use in connection with legal relations is, strictly speaking, figurative or fictional. The term 'transfer' is a good example. If X says that he has transferred his watch to Y, he may conceivably mean, quite literally, that he has physically handed over the watch to Y; or, more likely, that he has 'transferred' his *legal interest*, without any delivery of possession, - the latter, of course, being a relatively figurative use of possession, - the latter, of course, being a relatively figurative use of the term. This point will be reached again, when we come to treat of the 'transfer' of legal interests. As another instance of this essentially metaphorical use of a term borrowed from the physical world, the word 'power' may be mentioned. In legal discourse, as in daily life, it may frequently be used in the sense of physical or mental capacity to do a thing; but, more usually and aptly, it is used to indicate a '*legal* power,' the same observations apply, *mutatis mutandis*, to the term 'liberty.'

Passing to the field of contracts, we soon discover a similar inveterate tendency to confuse and blur legal discussions by failing to discriminate between the mental and physical facts involved in the so-called 'agreement' of the parties, and the legal 'contractual obligation' to which those facts give rise. Such ambiguity and confusion are peculiarly incident to the sue of the term 'contract.' One moment the word may mean *the agreement* of the parties; and then, with a rapid and unexpected shift, the writer or speaker may use the term to indicate the contractual obligation created by law as a result of the agreement.

The distinction between the agreement of the parties on the one hand, and, on the other, the legal obligation (or aggregate of present and potential legal rights, privileges, powers and immunities, etc.) is clearly recognized and forcefully stated in *Aycock* v *Martin*:

> The obligation then is not the contract,[21] is not in the contract, nor does it constitute any one of its terms, nor is it equivalent to all the terms united ... when the contract is made, the existing, binding law, whatever it may be, being the obligation on promisor to perform his undertaking, *eo instanti* attaches ... The terms of the contract are made alone by the parties to the agreement ... The obligation is the creature of law, - is the law existing when the contract is made, binding to the performance of the promise, and is furnished solely by society.[22]

Further instances of this sort of ambiguity will be noticed as the discussion proceeds.

Operative Facts Contrasted with Evidential Facts

For the purpose of subsequent convenient reference, it seems necessary at this point to lay emphasis upon another important distinction inherent to the very nature of things. The facts important in relation to a given jural transaction may be either *operative* facts or *evidential* facts. Operative, constitutive, causal, or dispositive facts are those which, under the general legal rules that are applicable, suffice to change legal relations, that is, either to create a new relation, or to extinguish an old one, or to perform both of these functions simultaneously.[23] For example, in the creation of a contractual obligation between A and B, the *affirmative* operative facts are, *inter alia*, that each of the parties is a human being, that each of them has lived for not less than a certain period of time (is not 'under age'), that A has made an 'offer,' that B has 'accepted' it, etc. It is sometimes necessary to consider, also, what may, from the particular point of view, be regarded as *negative* operative facts. Thus, e.g. the fact that A did not wilfully misrepresent an important matter to B, and the fact that A had not 'revoked' his offer, must really be included as parts of the totality of operative facts in the case already put.

Taking another example, - this time from the general field of torts - if A commits an assault on Y by putting the latter in fear of bodily harm, this particular group of facts immediately creates in Y the privilege of self-defense, - that is, the privilege of using sufficient force to repel X's attack; or, correlatively, the otherwise existing duty of Y to refrain from the application of force to the person of A is, by virtue of the special operative facts, immediately terminated or extinguished.

In passing, it may not be amiss to notice that the term, 'facts in issue,' is sometimes used in the present connection. If, as is usual, the term means 'facts put in issue by the *pleadings*,' the expression is an unfortunate one. The operative facts alleged by the pleadings are more or less *generic* in character; and if the pleadings be sufficient, only such *generic* operative facts are 'put in issue.' The operative facts of real life are, on the other hand, very specific. That being so, it is clear that the *real* and *specific* facts finally relied on are comparatively seldom put in issue by the pleadings. Thus, if, in an action of tort, the declaration of A alleges that he was, through the carelessness, etc., of B, bitten by the latter's dog, the fact alleged is generic in character, and it matters not whether it was dog Jim or dog Dick that did the biting. Even assuming, therefore, that the biting was done by Jim rather than by Dick, it could not be said that this specific fact was put in issue by the pleadings. Similarly, and more obviously, the pleading in an ordinary action involving so-called negligence, is usually very generic in character,[24] so that any one of various possible groups of specific operative facts would suffice, so far as the defendant's obligations *ex delicto* is concerned. It therefore could not be said that any one of such groups had been put in issue by the pleadings. A common fallacy in this connection is to regard the *specific* operative facts established in a given case as being but 'evidence' of the generic (or 'ultimate') operative facts alleged in the pleadings.[25]

An evidential fact is one which, on being ascertained, affords some logical basis - not conclusive - for inferring some other fact. The latter may be either a constitutive fact or an intermediate evidential fact. Of all the facts to be ascertained by the tribunal, the operative are, of course, of primary importance; the evidential are subsidiary in their functions.[26] As a rule there is little danger of confusing evidential facts with operative facts. But there is one type of case that not infrequently gives rise to this sort of error. Suppose that in January last a contractual obligation was created by written agreement passing between A and B. In an action now pending between these parties, the physical *instrument* is offered for inspection by the tribunal. If one were thoughtless, he would be apt to say that this is a case where part of the operative facts creating the original obligation are directly presented to the senses of the tribunal. Yet a moment's reflection will show that such is not the case. The document, in its then existing shape, had, as regards its operative effect, spent its force as soon as it was delivered in January last. If, therefore, the unaltered document is produced for inspection, the facts thus ascertained must, as regards the alleged contractual agreement, be purely evidential in character. That is to say, the present existence of the piece of paper, its specific tenor, etc., may, along with other evidential facts (relating to absence of change) tend to prove the various operative facts of last January, - to wit, that such paper existed at that time; that its tenor was then the same as it now is; that it was delivered by A to B, and so forth.

It now remains to observe that in many situations a single convenient term is employed to designate (generically) certain miscellaneous groups of operative facts which, though differing widely as to their individual 'ingredients,' have, as regards a given matter, the same *net* force and effect. When employed with discrimination, the term 'possession' is a word of this character; so also the term 'capacity,' the term 'domicile.' etc. But the general tendency to confuse legal and non-legal quantities is manifest here as elsewhere; so that only too frequently these words are used rather nebulously to indicate legal relations as such.[27]

Fundamental Jural Relations Contrasted with One Another

One of the greatest hindrances to the clear understanding, the incisive statement, and the true solution of legal problems frequently arises from the express or tacit assumption that all legal relations may be reduced to 'rights' and 'duties,' and that these latter categories are therefore adequate for the purpose of analyzing even the most complex legal interests, such as trusts, options, escrows, 'future' interests, corporate interests, etc. Even if the difficulty related merely to inadequacy and ambiguity of terminology, its seriousness would nevertheless be worthy of definite recognition and persistent effort toward improvement; for in any close reasoned problem, whether legal or non-legal, chameleon-hued words are a peril both to clear thought and to lucid expression.[28] As a matter of fact, however, the above mentioned inadequacy and ambiguity of terms unfortunately reflect, all too often, corresponding paucity and confusion as regards actual legal conceptions. That this is so may appear in some measure from the discussion to follow.

The strictly fundamental legal relations are, after all, *sui generis*; and thus it is that attempts at formal definition are always unsatisfactory, if not altogether useless. Accordingly, the most promising line of procedure seems to consist in exhibiting all of the various relations in a scheme of 'opposites' and 'correlatives,' and then proceedings to exemplify their individual scope and application in concrete cases. An effort will be made to pursue this method:

	(right	privilege	power	immunity
Jural Opposites	(			
	(no-right	duty	disability	liability
	(right	privilege	power	immunity
Jural Correlatives	(			
	(duty	no-right	liability	disability

Rights and Duties

As already intimated, the term 'rights' tends to be used indiscriminately to cover what in a given case may be a privilege, a power, or an immunity, rather than a right in the strictest sense; and this looseness of usage is occasionally recognised by the authorities. As said by Mr Justice Strong in *People* v *Dikeman*:

> The Word 'right' is defined by lexicographers to denote, among other things, *property*, *interest*, *power*, *prerogative*, *immunity*, *privilege* (Walker's Dict. Word 'Right'). In law it is most frequently applied to property in its restricted sense, but it is often used to designate *power*, *prerogative*, and *privilege.*[29]

Recognition of this ambiguity is also found in the language of Mr Justice Jackson, in *United States* v *Patrick*:

> The words 'right' or 'privilege' have, of course, a variety of meanings, according to the connection or context in which they are used. Their definition, as given by standard lexicographers, include 'that which one has a *legal claim to do*,' '*legal power*,' '*authority*,' '*immunity* granted by authority,' 'the investiture with special or peculiar rights.[30]

And, similarly, in the language of Mr Justice Sneed, in *Lonas* v *State*:

> The state, then, is forbidden from making and enforcing any law which shall abridge the *privileges* and *immunities* of citizens of the United States. It is said that the words *rights*, *privileges* and *immunities*, are abusively used, as if they were synonymous. The word *rights* is generic, common, embracing whatever may be lawfully claimed.[31]

It is interesting to observe, also, that a tendency toward discrimination may be found in a number of important constitutional and statutory provisions. Just how accurate the distinctions in the mind of the draftsman may have been it is, of course, impossible to say.[32]

Recognizing, as we must, the very broad and indiscriminate use of the term 'right,' what clue do we find, in ordinary legal discourse toward limiting the word in question to a definite and appropriate meaning? That clue lies in the correlative 'duty,' for it is certain that even those who use the word and the conception 'right' in the broadest possible way are accustomed to thinking of 'duty' as the invariable correlative. As said in *Lake Shore and M S R Co* v *Kurtz*:[33]

> A duty or a legal obligation is that which one ought or ought not to do. 'Duty' and 'right' are correlative terms. When a right is invaded, a duty is violated.[34]

In other words, if X has a right against Y that he shall stay off the former's land, the correlative (and equivalent) is that Y is under a duty toward X to stay off the place. If, as seems desirable, we should seek a synonym for the term 'right' in this limited and proper meaning, perhaps the word 'claim' would prove the best. The latter has the advantage of being a monosyllable.[35] In this connection, the language of Lord Watson in *Studd* v *Cook* is instructive:

> Any words which in a settlement of moveables would be recognized by the law of Scotland as sufficient to create a right or claim in favor of an executor ... must receive effect if used with reference to lands in Scotland.[36]

Privileges and 'No-Rights'

As indicated in the above scheme of jural relations, a privilege is the opposite of a duty, and the correlative of a 'no-right.' In the example last put, whereas X has a *right* or *claim* that Y, the other man, should stay off the land, he himself has the *privilege* of entering on the land; or, in equivalent words, X does not have a duty to stay off. The privilege of entering is the negation of a duty to stay off. As indicated by this case, some caution is necessary at this point; for, always, when it is said that a given privilege is the mere negation of a *duty*, what is meant, of course, is a duty having a content or tenor precisely *opposite* to that of the privilege in question. Thus, if, for some special reason, X has contracted with Y to go on the former's own land, it is obvious that X has, as regards Y, both the privilege of entering and the *duty of entering*. The privilege is perfectly consistent with this sort of duty, for the latter is of the *same* content or tenor as the privilege; but it still holds good that, as regards Y, X's privilege of entering is the precise negation of a duty to stay off. Similarly, if A has not contracted with B to perform certain work for the latter, A's privilege of *not* doing so is the very negation of a duty of *doing* so. Here again the duty contrasted is of a content or tenor exactly opposite to that of the privilege.

Passing now to the question of 'correlatives,' it will be remembered, of course, that a duty is the invariable correlative of that legal relation which is most property called a right or claim. That being so, if further evidence be needed as to the fundamental and important difference between a right (or claim) and a privilege, surely it is found in the fact that the correlative of the latter relation is a 'no-right,' there being no single term available to express the latter conception. Thus, the correlative of X's right that Y shall not enter on the land is Y's duty not to enter; but the correlative of X's privilege of entering himself is manifestly Y's 'no-right' that X shall not enter.

In view of the considerations thus far emphasized, the importance of keeping the conception of a right (or claim) and the conception of a privilege quite distinct from each other seems evident; and, more than that, it is equally clear that there should be a separate term to represent the latter relation. No doubt, as already indicated, it is very common to use the term 'right' indiscriminately, even when the relation designated is really that of privilege;[37] and only too often this identity of terms has involved for the particular speaker or writer a confusion or blurring of ideas. Good instances of this may be found even in unexpected places. Thus Professor Holland, in his work on *Jurisprudence*, referring to a different and well-known sort of ambiguity inherent in the Latin '*Ius*,' the Herman '*Recht*,' the Italian '*Diritto*,' and the French '*Droit*.' - terms to express 'not only 'a right,' but also 'Law' in the abstract,' - very aptly observes:

> If the expression of widely different ideas by one and the same term resulted only in the necessity for … clumsy paraphrases, or obviously inaccurate paraphrases, no great harm would be done; but unfortunately the identity of terms seems irresistibly to suggest an identity between the ideas expressed by them.[38]

Curiously enough, however, in the very chapter where this appears - the chapter on 'Rights,' - the notions of right, privilege, and power seem to be blended, and that too, although the learned author states that 'the correlative of … legal right is legal duty,' and that 'these pairs of terms express … in each case the same state of facts viewed from opposite sides.' While the whole chapter must be read in order to appreciate the seriousness of this lack of discrimination, a single passage must suffice by way of example:

> If … the power of the State will protect him in so carrying out his wishes, and will compel such acts or forbearances on the part of other people as may be necessary in order that his wishes may be so carried out, then he has a 'legal right' so to carry out his wishes.[39]

The first part of this passage suggests privileges, the middle part rights (or claims), and the last part privileges.[40]

Similar difficulties seem to exist in Professor Gray's able and entertaining work on *The Nature and Sources of Law*. In his chapter on 'Legal Rights and Duties' the distinguished author takes the position that a right always has a duty as its correlative;[41] and he seems to define the former relation substantially according to the more limited meaning of 'claim.' Legal privileges, powers, and immunities are *prima facie* ignored, and the impression conveyed that all legal relations can be comprehended under the conceptions 'right' and 'duty.' But, with the greatest hesitation and deference, the suggestion may be ventured that a number of his examples seem to show the inadequacy of such mode of treatment. Thus, e.g. he says:

> The eating of shrimp salad is an interest of mine, and, if I can pay for it, the law will protect that interest, and it is therefore a right of mine

> to eat shrimp salad which I have paid for, although I know that shrimp salad always gives me the colic.[42]

This passage seems to suggest primarily two classes of relations: *first*, the party's respective privileges, as against A, B, C, D and others in relation to rating the salad, or, correlatively, the respective 'no-rights' of A, B, C, D and others that the party should not eat the salad; *second*, the party's respective rights (or claims) as against A, B, C, D and others that they should interfere with the physical act of eating the salad, or, correlatively, the respective duties of A, B, C, D and others that they should not interfere.

These two groups of relations seem perfectly distinct; and the privileges could, in a given case, exist even though the rights mentioned did not. A, B, C, and D, being the owners of the salad, might say to X: 'Eat the salad, if you can; you have our license to do so, but we don't agree not to interfere with you.' In such a case the privileges exist, so that if X succeeds in eating the salad, he has violated no rights of any of the parties. But it is equally clear that if A had succeeded in holding so fast to the dish that X couldn't eat the contents, no right of X would have been violated.[43]

Perhaps the essential character and importance of the distinction can be shown by a slight variation of the facts. Suppose that X, being already the legal owner of the salad, contracts with Y that he (X) will never eat this particular food. With A, B, C, D and others no such contract has been made. One of the relations now existing between X and Y is, as a consequence, fundamentally different from the relation between X and A. As regards Y, X has no privilege of eating the salad; but as regards A or any of the others, X has such a privilege. It is to be observed incidentally that X's right that Y should not eat the food persists even though X's own privilege of doing so has been extinguished.'[44]

On grounds already emphasized, it would seem that the line of reasoning pursued by Lord Lindley in the great case of *Quinn* v *Leathem* is deserving of comment:

> The plaintiff had the ordinary *rights* of the British subject. He was at *liberty* to earn his living in how own way, provided he did not violate some special law prohibiting him from so doing, and provided he did not infringe the rights of other people. This *liberty* involved *the liberty* to deal with other persons who were willing to deal with him. *This liberty* is a *right* recognized by law; its *correlative* is the general *duty* of every one not to prevent the free exercise of this *liberty*

> except so far as his own liberty of action may justify him in so doing. But a person's *liberty* or *right* to deal with others is nugatory unless they are at liberty to deal with him if they choose to do so. Any interference with their liberty to deal with him affects him.[45]

A 'liberty' considered as a legal relation (or 'right' in the loose and generic sense of that term) must mean, if it have any definite content at all, precisely the same thing as *privilege*;[46] and certainly that is the fair connotation of the term as used the first three times in the passage quoted. It is equally clear, as already indicated, that such a privilege or liberty to deal with others at will might very conceivably exist without any peculiar concomitant rights against 'third parties' as regards certain kinds of interference.[47] Whether there should be such concomitant rights (or claims) is ultimately a question of justice and policy; and it should be considered, as such, on its merits. The only correlative logically implied by the privileges or liberties in question are the 'no-rights' of 'third parties.' It would therefore be a *non sequitur* to conclude from the mere existence of such liberties that 'third parties' are under a *duty* not to interfere, etc. Yet in the middle of the above passage from Lord Lindley's opinion there is a sudden and question-begging shift in the use of terms. First, the 'liberty' in question is transmuted into a 'right'; and then, possibly under the seductive influence of the latter work, it is assumed that the 'correlative' must be 'the general duty of every one not to prevent, etc.[48]

Another interesting and instructive example may be taken from Lord Bowen's oft-quoted opinion in *Mogul Steamship Co* v *McGregor*:

> We are presented in this case with an apparent conflict or antinomy between two rights that are equally regarded by the law - the right of the plaintiffs to be protected in the legitimate exercise of their trade, and the right of the defendants to carry on their business as seems best to them, provided they commit no wrong to others.[49]

As the learned judge states, the conflict or antinomy is only apparent; but this fact seems to be obscured by the very indefinite and rapidly shifting meanings with which the term 'right' is used in the above quoted language. Construing the passage as a whole, it seems plain enough that by 'the right of the plaintiffs' in relation to the defendants a legal right or claim in the strict sense must be meant; whereas by 'the right of the defendants' in relation to the plaintiffs a legal privilege must be intended. That being so, the 'two rights' mentioned in the beginning of the passage, being respectively claim and privilege, could not be in conflict with each other. To the extent that the defendants have privileges the plaintiffs have no rights; and, conversely, to the extent that the plaintiffs have rights the defendants have no privileges ('no-privilege' equals duty of opposite tenor).[50]

Thus far it has been assumed that the term 'privilege' is the most appropriate and satisfactory to designate the mere negation of duty. Is there good warrant for this?

In Mackeldey's *Roman Law* it is said:

> Positive laws either contain general principles embodied in the rules of law ... or for especial reasons they establish something that differs from those general principles. In the first case they contain a common law (*jus commune*), in the second a special law (*jus singulare s. exorbitans*). The latter is either favorable or unfavorable ... according as it enlarges or restricts, in opposition to the common rule the rights of those for whom it is established. The favorable special law (*jus singulare*) as also the right created by it ... in the Roman law is termed benefit of the law (*beneficium juris*) or privilege (*privilegium*).[51]

First a special law, and then by association of ideas, a special advantage conferred by such a law. With such antecedents, it is not surprising that the English word 'privilege' is not infrequently used, even at the present time, in the sense of a special or peculiar legal advantage (whether right, privilege, power or immunity) belonging either to some individual or to some particular class of persons.[52] There are, indeed, a number of judicial opinions recognizing this as one of the meanings of the term in question.[53] That the word has a wider signification even in ordinary non-technical usage is sufficiently indicated, however, by the fact that the term '*special* privileges' is so often used to indicate a contrast to ordinary or general privileges. More than this, the dominant specific connotation of the term as used in popular speech seems to be mere *negation of duty*. This is manifest in the terse and oft-repeated expression, 'That is your privilege,' - meaning, of course, 'You are under no duty to do otherwise.'

Such being the case, it is not surprising to find, from a wide survey of judicial precedents, that the *dominant* technical meaning of the term is, similarly, negation of *legal duty*.[54] There are two very common examples of this, relating respectively to 'privileged communications' in the law of libel and to 'privileges against self-crimination' in the law of evidence. As regards the first case, it is elementary that if a certain group of operative facts are present, a privilege exists which, without such facts, would not be recognized.[55] It is, of course, equally clear that even though all such facts be present as last supposed, the superadded fact of malice will, in cases of so-called 'conditional' privilege,' negative the privilege that otherwise would exist. It must be evident also, that whenever the privilege does exist, it is not special in the sense of arising from a special law, or of being conferred as a special favor on a particular individual. The same privilege would exist, by virtue of general rules, for any person whatever under similar circumstances. So, also, in the law of evidence, the privilege against self-crimination signifies the mere negation of a duty to testify, - a duty which rests upon a witness in relation to all ordinary matters; and, quite obviously, such privilege arises, if at all, only by virtue of general laws.[56]

As already intimated, while both the conception and the term 'privilege' find conspicuous exemplification under the law of libel and the law of evidence, they nevertheless have a much wider significance and utility as a matter of judicial usage. To make this clear, a few miscellaneous judicial precedents will now be noticed. In *Dowman's Case*, decided in the year 1583, and reported by Coke, the court applied the term to the subject of waste:

> And as to the objection which was made, that the said privilege to be without impeachment of waste can not be without deed, etc. To that it was answered and resolved, that if it was admitted that a deed in such case should be requisite, yet without question all the estates limited would be good, although it is admitted, that the clause concerning the said privilege would be void.[57]

In the great case of *Allen* v *Flood* the opinion of Mr Justice Hawkins furnishes a useful passage for the purpose now in view:

> Every person has a privilege ...in the interests of public justice to put the criminal law in motion against another whom he *bona fide*, and upon reasonable and probable cause, believes to have been guilty of a crime ... It must not, however, be supposed that hatred and ill-will existing in the mind of a prosecutor must of necessity *destroy* the *privilege*, for it is not impossible that such hatred and ill-will may have very natural and pardonable reasons for existing.[58]

Applying the term in relation to the subject of property, Mr Justice Foster, of the Supreme Court of Maine, said in the case of *Pulitzer* v *Livingston*:

> It is contrary to the policy of the law that there should be any outstanding titles, estates, or powers, by the existence, operation or exercise of which, at a period of time beyond lives in being and twenty-one years and a fraction thereafter, the complete and unfettered enjoyment of an estate, *with all the rights, privileges and powers incident to ownership*, should be qualified or impeded.[59]

As a final example in the present connection, the language of Baron Alderson in *Hilton* v *Eckerley* may be noticed:

> *Prima facie* it is the privilege of a trader in a free country, in all matters not contrary to law, to regulate his own mode of carrying them on according to his discretion and choice.[60]

The closest synonym of legal 'privilege' seems to be legal 'liberty' or legal 'freedom.'[61] This is sufficiently indicated by an unusually discriminating and instructive passage in Mr Justice Cave's opinion in *Allen* v *Flood*:

> The personal rights with which we are most familiar are: 1. Rights of reputation; 2. Rights of bodily safety and freedom; 3. Rights of property; or, in other words, rights relating to mind, body and estate ... In my subsequent remarks the word 'right' will, as far as possible, always be used in the above sense; and it is the more necessary to insist on this as during the argument at your Lordship's bar it was frequently used in a much wider and more indefinite sense. Thus it was said that a man has a perfect right to fire off a gun, when all that was meant, apparently, was that a man has a *freedom* or *liberty* to fire off a gun, so long as he does not violate or infringe any one's rights in doing so, which is a very different thing from a right, the violation or disturbance of which can be remedied or prevented by legal process.[62]

While there are numerous other instances of the apt use of the term 'liberty,' both in judicial opinions[63] and in conveyancing documents,[64] it is by no means so common or definite a word as 'privilege.' The former term is far more likely to be used in the sense of physical or personal freedom (i.e., absence of physical restraint), as distinguished from a legal relation; and very frequently there is the connotation of *general* political liberty, as distinguished from a particular relation between two definite individuals. Besides all this, the term 'privilege' has the advantage of giving us, as a variable, the adjective 'privileged.' Thus, it is frequently convenient to speak of a privileged act, a privileged transaction, a privileged conveyance, etc.

The term 'license,' sometimes used as if it were synonymous with 'privilege,' is not strictly appropriate. This is simply another of those innumerable cases in which the mental and physical facts are so frequently confused with the legal relation which they create.[65] Accurately used, 'license' is a generic term to indicate a group of *operative* facts required to create a particular privilege, - this being especially evident when the word is used in the common phrase 'leave and license.' This point is brought out by a passage from Mr Justice Adams's opinion in *Clifford* v *O'Neill*:

> A license is mere a *permission* to do an act which, *without such permission*, would amount to a trespass ... nor will the continuous enjoyment of the *privilege conferred*, for a any period of time cause it to ripen into a tangible interest in the land affected.[66]

Powers and Liabilities

As indicated in the preliminary scheme of jural relations, a legal power (as distinguished, of course, from a mental or physical power) is the opposite of legal disability, and the correlative of legal liability. But what is the intrinsic nature of a legal power as such? Is it possible to analyze the conception represented by this constantly employed and very important term of legal discourse? Too close an analysis might seem metaphysical rather than useful; so that what is here presented is intended only as an approximate explanation, sufficient for all purposes.

A change in a given legal relation may result (1) from some superadded fact or group of facts not under the volitional control of a human being (or human beings); or (2) from some superadded fact or group of facts which are under the volitional control of one or more human beings. As regards the second class of cases, the person (or persons) whose volitional control is paramount may be said to have the (legal) power to effect the particular change of legal relations that is involved in the problem.

This second class of cases - powers in the technical sense - must now be further considered. The nearest synonym for any ordinary case seems to be (legal) 'ability,'[67] - the latter being obviously the opposite of 'inability,' or 'disability.' The term 'right,' so frequently and loosely used in the present connection is an unfortunate term for the purpose, - a not unusual result being confusion of thought as well as ambiguity of expression.[68] The term 'capacity' is equally unfortunate; for, as we have already seen, when used with discrimination, this word denotes a particular group of operative facts, and not a legal relation of any kind.

Many examples of legal powers may readily be given. Thus, X, the owner of ordinary personal property 'in a tangible object' has the power to extinguish his own legal interest (rights, powers, immunities, etc.) through that totality of operative facts known as abandonment; and - simultaneously and correlatively - to create in other persons privileges and powers relating to the abandoned object, - e.g. the power to acquire title to the latter by appropriating it.[69] *Similarly*, X has the power to transfer his interest to Y, - that is, to extinguish his own interest and concomitantly create in Y a new and corresponding interest.[70] So also X has the power to create contractual obligations of various kinds. Agency cases are likewise instructive. By the use of some *metaphorical* expression such as the Latin, *qui facit per alium, facit per se*, the true nature of an agency relations is only too frequently obscured. The creation of an agency relation involves, *inter alia*, the grant of legal powers to the so-called agent, and the creation of correlative liabilities in the principal.[71] That is to say, one party, P, has the power to create agency powers in another party, A, - for example, the power to convey P's property, the power to impose (so-called) contractual obligations on P, the power to discharge a debt owing to P, the power to 'receive' title to property so that it shall vest in P, and so forth. In passing, it may be well to observe that the term 'authority,' so frequently used in agency cases, is very ambiguous and slippery in its connotation. Properly employed in the present connection, the word seems to be an abstract or qualitative term corresponding to the concrete 'authorization,' - the latter consisting of a particular group of operative facts taking place between the principal and the agent. All too often, however, the term in question is so used as to blend and confuse these operative facts with the powers and privileges thereby created in the agent.[72] A careful discrimination in these particulars would, it is submitted, go far toward clearing up certain problems in the law of agency.[73]

Essentially similar to the powers of agents are powers of appointment in relation to property interests. So, too, the powers of public officers are, intrinsically considered, comparable to those of agents, - for example, the power of a sheriff to sell property under a writ of execution. The power of a donor, in a gift *causa mortis*, to revoke the gift and divest the title of the donee is another clear example of the legal quantities now being considered;[74] also a pledgee's statutory power of sale.[75]

There are, on the other hand, cases where the true nature of the relations involved has not, perhaps, been so clearly recognized. Thus, in the case of a conditional sale of personalty, assuming the vendee's agreement has been fully performed except as to the payment of the last instalment and the time for the latter has arrived, what is the interest of such vendee as regards the property? Has he, as so often assumed, merely a contractual *right* to have title passed to him by consent of the vendor, on final payment being made; or has he, irrespective of the consent of the vendor the power to divest the title of the latter and to acquire a perfect title for himself? Though the language of the cases is not always so clear as it might be, the vendee seems to have precisely that sort of power.[76] Fundamentally considered, the typical escrow transaction in which the performance of conditions is within the volitional control of the grantee, is somewhat similar to the conditional sale of personalty; and, when reduced to its lowest terms, the problem seems easily in terms of legal powers. Once the 'escrow' is formed, the grantor still has the legal title; but the grantee has an irrevocable power to divest that title by performance of certain conditions (i.e. the addition of various operative facts), and concomitantly to vest title in himself. While such power is outstanding, the grantor is, of course, subject to a correlative liability to have his title divested.[77] Similarly, in the case of a conveyance of land in fee simple subject to condition subsequent, after the condition has been performed, the original grantor is commonly said to have a 'right of entry.' If, however, the problem is analyzed, it will be seen that, as of primary importance, the grantor has two legal quantities, (1) the privilege of entering, and (2) the power by means of such entry, to divest the estate of the grantee.[78] The latter's estate endures, subject to the correlative liability of being divested, until such power is actually exercised.[79]

Passing now to the field of contracts, suppose A mails a letter to B offering to sell the former's land, Whiteacre, to the latter for ten thousand dollars, such letter being duly received. The operative facts thus far mentioned have created a power as regards B and a correlative liability as regards A. B, by dropping a letter of acceptance in the box, has the power to impose a potential or inchoate[80] *obligation ex contractu* on A and himself; and, assuming that the land is worth fifteen thousand dollars, that particular legal quantity - the 'power *plus* liability' relation between a and B - seems to be worth about five thousand dollars to B. The liability of A will continue for a reasonable time unless, in exercise of his power to do so, A previously extinguishes it by that series of operative facts known as 'revocation'. These last matters are usually described by saying that A's 'offer' will 'continue' or 'remain open' for a reasonable time, or for the definite time actually specified, unless A previously 'withdraws' or 'revokes' such offer.[81] While, no doubt, in the great majority of cases no harm results from the use of such expressions, yet these forms of statement seem to represent a blending of non-legal and legal quantities which, in any problem requiring careful reasoning, should preferably be kept distinct. An offer, considered as a series of physical and mental operative facts, has spent its force and becomes *functus officio* as soon as such series has been completed by the 'offerees's receipt'. The real question is therefore as to the *legal effect*, if any, at that moment of time. If the latter consist of B's power and A's correlative liability, manifestly it is those *legal relations* that 'continue' or 'remain open' until modified by revocation or other operative facts.[82] What has thus far been said concerning contracts completed by mail would seem to apply, *mutatis mutandis*, to every type of contract. Even where the parties are in the presence of each other, the offer creates a liability against the offerer, together with a correlative power in favor of the offeree. The only distinction for present purposes would be in the fact that such power and such liability would expire within a very short period of time.

Perhaps the practical justification for this method of analysis is somewhat greater in relation to the subject of opinions. In his able work on *Contracts*, Langdell says:

> If the offerer stipulates that his offer shall remain open for a specified time, the first question is whether such a stipulation constitutes a binding contract ... When such a stipulation is binding, the further question arises, whether it makes the offer irrevocable. It has been a common opinion that it does, but that is clearly a mistake. ... an offer is merely one of the element of a contract; and it is indispensable to the making of a contract that the wills of a contracting parties do, in legal contemplation, concur at the moment of making it. An offer, therefore, which the party making it has no power to revoke, is a legal impossibility. Moreover, if the stipulation should make the offer irrevocable, it would be a contract incapable of being broken; which is also a legal impossibility. The only effect, therefore, of such a stipulation is to give the offeree a claim for damages if the stipulation be broken by revoking the offer.[83]

The foregoing reasoning ignores the fact that an ordinary offer *ipso facto* creates a legal relation - a legal power and a legal liability, - and that it is this relation (rather than the physical and mental facts constituting the offer) that 'remains open.' If these points be conceded, there seems no difficulty in recognizing a unilateral option agreement supported by consideration or embodied in a sealed instrument as creating in the optionee an irrevocable power to create, at any time within the period specified, a bilateral obligation as between himself and the giver of the option. Correlatively to that power, there would, of course, be a liability against the option-giver which he himself would have no power to extinguish. The courts seem to have no difficulty in reaching precisely this result as a matter of substance; though their explanations are always in terms of 'withdrawal of offer,' and similar expressions savoring of physical and mental quantities.[84]

In connection with the powers and liabilities crated respectively by an ordinary offer and by an option, it is interesting to consider the liabilities of a person engaged in a 'public calling'; for, as it seems, such a party's characteristic position is, one might almost say, intermediate between that of an ordinary contractual offerer and that of an option-giver. It has indeed been usual to assert that such a party is (generally speaking) under a present *duty* to all other parties; but this is believed to be erroneous. Thus, Professor Wyman, in his work on *Public Service Companies*, says:

> The duty placed upon every one exercising a public calling is primarily *a duty* to serve every man who is a member of the public … It is somewhat difficult to place this exceptional duty in our legal system … The truth of the matter is that the obligation resting upon one who has undertaken the performance of public duty is *sui generis*.[85]

It is submitted that the learned writer's difficulties arise primarily from a failure to see that the innkeeper, the common carrier and others similarly 'holding out' are under present *liabilities* rather than present *duties*. Correlative to those liabilities are the respective powers of the various members of the public. Thus, for example, a traveling member of the public has the legal power, by making proper application and sufficient tender, to impose a duty on the innkeeper to receive him as a guest. For breach of the duty *thus* created an action would of course lie. It would therefore seem that the innkeeper is, to some extent, like one who had given an option to every traveling member of the public. He differs, as regards net effect, only because he can extinguish his present liabilities and the correlative powers of the traveling member of the public *by going out of business*. Yet, on the other hand, his liabilities are more onerous that that of an ordinary contractual offerer, for he cannot extinguish his liabilities by any simple performance akin to the revocation of offer. As regards all the 'legal powers' thus far considered, possibly some caution is necessary. If, for example, we consider the ordinary property owner's power of alienation, it is necessary to distinguish carefully between the *legal* power, the *physical* power to do the things necessary for the 'exercise' of the legal power, and, finally, the *privilege* of doing these things - that is, if such privilege does really exist. It may or may not. Thus, if X, a landowner, has contracted with Y that the former will not alienate to Z, the acts of X necessary to exercise the power of alienating to Z are privileged as between X and every party other than Y; but, obviously, as between X and Y, the former has no privilege of doing the necessary acts; or conversely, he is under a duty to Y not to do what is necessary to exercise the power.

In view of what has already been said, very little may suffice concerning a *liability* as such. The latter, as we have seen, if the correlative of power, and the opposite of immunity (or exemption). While no doubt the term 'liability' is often loosely used as a synonym for 'duty,' or 'obligation,' it is believed, from an extensive survey of judicial precedents, that the connotation already adopted as most appropriate to the word in question is fully justified. A few cases tending to indicate this will now be noticed. In *McNeer* v *McNeer*, Mr Justice Magruder balanced the conceptions of power and liability as follows:

> So long as she lived, however, his interest in her land lacked those elements of property, such as *power of disposition* and *liability to sale on* execution which had had formerly given it the character of a vested estate.[86]

In *Booth* v *Commonwealth*, the court had to construe a Virginia statute providing 'that all free white male persons who are twenty-one years of age and not over sixty, shall be liable to serve as jurors, except as hereinafter provided.' It is plain that this enactment imposed only a *liability* and not a *duty*. It is a liability to have a duty created. The latter would arise only when, in exercise of their powers, the parties litigant and the court officers had done what was necessary to impose a specific duty to perform the functions of a juror. The language of the court, by Moncure, J, is particularly apposite as indicating that liability is the opposite, or negative, of immunity (or exemption):

> The word both expressed and implied is 'liable,' which has a very different meaning from 'qualified' ... Its meaning is 'bound' or 'obliged.' ... A person exempt from serving on juries is not liable to serve, and a person not liable to serve is exempt from serving. The terms seem to be convertible.[87]

A further good example of judicial usage is to be found in *Emery* v *Clough.* Referring to a gift *causa mortis* and the donee's liability to have his already vested interest divested by the donor's exercise of his power of revocation, Mr Justice Smith said:

> The title to the gift *causa mortis* passed by the delivery, defeasible only in the lifetime of the donor, and his death perfects the title in the donee by terminating the donor's right or *power of defeasance.* The property passes from the donor to the donee directly ... and after his death it is *liable* to be *divested* only in favor of the donor's creditors ... His right and power ceased with his death. [88]

Perhaps the nearest synonym of 'liability' is 'subjection' or 'responsibility.' As regards the latter word, a passage from Mr Justice Day's opinion in *McElfresh* v *Kirkendall* is interesting:

> The words 'debt' and 'liability' are not synonymous, and they are not commonly so understood. As applied to the pecuniary relations of the parties, liability is a term of broader significance than debt. ... Liability is responsibility.[89]

While the term in question has the broad generic connotation already indicated, no doubt it very frequently indicates that specific form of liability (or complex of liabilities) that is correlative to a power (or complex of powers)[90] vested in a party litigant and the various court officers. Such was held to be the meaning of a certain California statute involved in the case of *Lattin* v *Gillette.*[91] Said Mr Justice Harrison:

> The word 'liability' is the condition in which an individual is placed after a breach of his contract, or a violation of any obligation resting upon him. It is defined by Bouvier to be responsibility.[92]

Immunities and Disabilities

As already brought out, immunity is the correlative of disability ('no-power'), and the opposite, or negation, of liability. Perhaps it will also be plain, from the preliminary outline and from the discussion down to this point, that a power bears the same general contrast to an immunity that a right does to a privilege. A right is one's affirmative claim against another, and a privilege is one's freedom from the right or claim of another. Similarly, a power is one's affirmative 'control' over a given legal relation as against another; whereas an immunity is one's freedom from the legal power or 'control' of another as regards some legal relation.

A few examples may serve to make this clear. X, a landowner, has, as we have seen, power to alienate to Y or to any other ordinary party. On the other hand, X has also various immunities as against Y, an all other ordinary parties. For Y is under a disability (i.e. he has no power) so far as shifting the legal interest either to himself or to a third party is concerned; and what is true of Y applies similarly to every one else who has not by virtue of special operative facts acquired a power to alienate X's property. If, indeed, a sheriff has been duly empowered by a write of execution to sell X's interest, that is a very different matter: correlative to such sheriff's power would be the *liability* of X, - the very opposite of immunity (or exemption). It is elementary, too, that as against the sheriff, X might be immune or exempt in relation to certain parcels of property, and be liable as to others.[93] Similarly, if an agent has been duly appointed by X to sell a given piece of property, then, as to the latter, X has, in relation to such agent, a liability rather than an immunity.

For over a century there has been, in this country, a great deal of important litigation involving immunities from powers of taxation. If there be any lingering misgivings as to the 'practical' importance of accuracy and discrimination in legal conceptions and legal terms, perhaps some of such doubts would be dispelled by considering the numerous cases on valuable taxation exemptions coming before the United States Supreme Court. Thus, in *Phoenix Ins. Co* v *Tennessee*, Mr Justice Peckham expressed the views of the court as follows:

> In granting to the De Soto Company 'all the rights, privileges, and immunities' of the Bluff City Company, all words are used which could be regarded as necessary to carry the exemption from taxation possessed by the Bluff City Company; while in the next following grant, that of the charter of the plaintiff in error, the word 'immunity'

> is omitted. Is there any meaning to be attached to that omission, and if so, what? We think some meaning is to be attached to it. The word 'immunity' expresses more clearly and definitely an intention to include therein an exemption from taxation than does either of the other words. Exemption from taxation is more accurately described as an 'immunity' than as a privilege, although it is not to be denied that the latter word may sometimes and under some circumstances include such exemptions.[94]

In *Morgan* v *Louisiana*, there is an instructive discussion from the pen of Mr, Justice Field. In holding that on a foreclosure sale of the franchise and property of a railroad an immunity from taxation did not pass to the purchaser, the learned judge said:

> As has been often said by this court, the whole community is interested in retaining the power of taxation undiminished ... The exemption of the property of the company from taxation, and the exemption of its officers and servants from jury and military duty, were both intended for the benefit of the company, and its benefit alone. In their personal character they are analogous to exemptions from execution of certain property of debtors, made by laws of several of the states.[95]

So far as immunities are concerned, the two judicial discussions last quoted concern respectively problems of interpretation and problems of alienability. In many other cases difficult constitutional questions have arisen as the result of statutes impairing or extending various kinds of immunities. Litigants have, from time to time, had occasion to appeal both to the clause against impairment of the obligation of contracts and to the provision against depriving a person of property without due process of law. This has been especially true as regards exemptions from taxation[96] and exemptions from execution.[97]

If a word may now be permitted with respect to mere terms as such, the first thing to note is that the word 'right' is overworked in the field of immunities as elsewhere.[98] As indicated, however, by the judicial expressions already quoted, the best synonym is, of course, the term 'exemption'.[99] It is instructive to note, also, that the word 'impunity' has a very similar connotation. This is made evident by the interesting discriminations of Lord Chancellor Finch in *Skelton* v *Skelton*, a case decided in 1677:

> But this I would by no means allow, that equity should enlarge the restraints of the disabilities introduced by act of parliament; and as to the granting of injunctions to stay waste, I took a distinction where tenant hath only *impunitatem*, and where he hath *jus in arboribus*. If the tenant have only a bare indemnity or *exemption* from an action (at law), if he committed waste, there it is fit he should be restrained by injunction from committing it.[100]

In the latter part of the preceding discussion, eight conceptions of the law have been analyzed and compared in some detail, the purpose having been to exhibit not only their intrinsic meaning and scope, but also their relations to one another and the methods by which they are applied, in judicial reasoning, to the solution of concrete problems of litigation. Before concluding this branch of the discussion a general suggestion may be ventured as to that great practical importance of a clear appreciation of the distinctions and discriminations set forth. If a homely metaphor be permitted, these eight conceptions, - rights and duties, privileges and no-rights, powers and liabilities, immunities and disabilities, - seem to be what may be called 'the lowest common denominators of the law.' Ten fractions (1-3, 2-5, etc.) may, *superficially*, seem so different from one another as to defy comparison. If, however, they are expressed in terms of their lowest common denominators (5-15, 6-15, etc.), comparison becomes easy, and fundamental similarity may be discovered. The same thing is of course true as regards the lowest generic conceptions to which any and all 'legal quantities' may be reduced.

Reverting, for example, to the subject of powers, it might be difficult at first glance to discover any essential and fundamental similarity between conditional sales of personalty, escrow transactions, option agreements, agency relations, powers of appointment, etc. But if all these relations are reduced to their lowest generic terms, the conceptions of legal power and legal liability are seen to be dominantly, though not exclusively, applicable throughout the series. By such a process it becomes possible not only to discover essential similarities and illuminating analogies in the midst of what appears superficially to be infinite and hopeless variety, but also to discern common principles of justice and policy underlying the various jural problems involved. An indirect, yet very practical, consequence is that it frequently becomes feasible, by virtue of such analysis, to use as persuasive authorities judicial precedents that might otherwise seem altogether irrelevant. If this point be valid with respect to powers, it would seem to be equally so as regards all of the other basic conceptions of the law. In short, the deeper the analysis, the greater becomes one's perception of fundamental unity and harmony in the law.[101]

Notes

1 F Bacon, *Uses* (circa 1602) Rowe's edn (1806) 5-6:

> The nature of an use is best discerned by considering what it is not, and then what it is ... First, an use is no right, title, or interest in law; and therefore master attorney, who read upon this statute, said well, that there are but two rights: *Jus in re*: *Jus ad rem* ... The one is an estate, which is jus in re; the other a demand, which is *jus ad rem*, but an use is neither ... So as now we are come by negatives to the affirmative, what an use is ... *Usus est dominium fiducarium*: Use is an ownership in trust ... So that *usus and status, sive possessio, potius differunt secundum rationem fori, quam secundum, naturum rei*, for that one of them is in court of law, the other in court of conscience.

2 E Coke, *First Part of the Institutes of the Laws of England* (1628) sec 464:

> *Nota*, an use is a trust or confidence reposed in some other, which is not issuing out of the land, but as a thing collateral, annexed in privitie to the estate of the land, and to the person touching the land, *scilicet*, that *cesty que use* shall take the profit, and that the terre-tenant shall make an estate according to his direction. So as *cesty que use* had neither *jus in re*, nor *jus ad rem*, but only a confidence and trust for which he had no remedie by the common law, but for the breach of trust, his remedie was only by subpoena in chancerie.

This definition is quoted and discussed approvingly in T Lewin, *Trusts*, 12th edn (1911) 1. It is also noticed in FW Maitland, *Lectures on Equity* (1909) 43, 116.

3 See Langdell, 'Classification of Rights and Wrongs' (1900) 13 *Harvard Law Review* 659, 673:

> Can equity then create such rights as it finds to be necessary for the purposes of justice? As equity wields only physical power it seems to be impossible that it should actually create anything ... It seems, therefore, that equitable rights exist only in contemplation of equity, i.e., that they are a fiction invented by equity for the promotion of justice ... Shutting our eyes, then, to the fact that equitable rights are a fiction and assuming them to have an actual existence, what is their nature, what their extent and what is the field which they occupy? ... They must not violate the law ... Legal and equitable rights must, therefore, exist side by side, and the latter cannot interfere with, or in any manner effect, the former.

See also Langdell, 'A Brief Survey of Equity Jurisdiction' (1887) 1 *Harvard Law Review* 55, 60:

> Upon the whole, it may be said that equity could not create rights *in rem* if it would, and that would not if it could.

Compare *ibid* 58 and CC Langdell, *Summary of Equity Pleading*, 2nd edn (1883) secs 45, 182-184.

4 See Ames, 'Purchase for Value Without Notice' (1887) 1 *Harvard Law Review* 1, 9:

> The trustee is the owner of the land, and, of course, two persons with adverse interests cannot be owners of the same thing. What the cestui que trust really owns is the obligation of the trustee; for an obligation is as truly the subject matter of property as any physical res. The most striking difference between property in a thing and property in an obligation is in the mode of enjoyment. The owner of a house or a horse enjoys the fruits of ownership without the aid of any other person. The only way in which the owner of an obligation can realize his ownership is by compelling its performance by the obligor. Hence, in the one case, the owner is said to have a right in rem, and in the other, a right in personam. In other respects the common rules of property apply equally to ownership of things and ownership of obligations. For example, what may be called the passive rights of ownership are the same in both cases. The general duty resting on all mankind not to destroy the property of another, is as cogent in favor of an obligee as it is in favor of the owner of a horse. And the violation of this duty is as pure a tort in the one case as in the other.

5 FW Maitland , *Lectures on Equity* (1909) 17, 18, 112:

> The thesis that I have to maintain is this, that equitable estates and interests are not *jura in rem*. For reasons that we shall perceive by and by, they have come to look very much like jura in rem; but just for this very reason it is the more necessary for us to observe that they are essentially jura in personam, not rights against the world at large, but rights against certain persons'.

See also Maitland, 'Trust and Corporation' (1904) reprinted in FW Maitland, *Collected Papers* (1911) vol. 3, 321, 325.

6 J Austin, *Lectures on Jurisprudence*, 5th edn (1885) vol. 1, 378:

> By the provisions of that part of the English law which is called equity, a contract to sell at once vests *jus in rem* or ownership in the buyer, and the seller has only jus in *re aliena* ... To complete the transaction the legal interest of the seller must be passed to the buyer, in legal form. To this purpose the buyer has only jus in personam: a right to compel the seller to pass his legal interest; but speaking generally, he has *dominium* or *jus in rem*, and the instrument is a conveyance.

7 JW Salmond, *Jurisprudence*, 2nd edn (1907) 230:

> If we have regard to the essence of the matter rather than to the form of it a trustee is not an owner at all, but a mere agent, upon whom the law has conferred the power and imposed the duty of administering the property of another person. In legal theory, however, he is not a mere agent, but an owner. He is a person to whom the property of someone else is fictitiously attributed by the law, to the intent hat the rights and powers thus vested in a nominal owner shall be used by him on behalf of the real owner.

8 See Walter G Hart (author of *Digest of Law of Trusts*) 'The Place of Trust in Jurisprudence' (1912) 28 *Law Quarterly Review* 290, 296. His position is substantially that of Ames and Maitland.

At the end of the article Sir Frederick Pollock, the editor, puts the query: 'Why is Trust not entitled to rank as a head *sui generis*?'

9 See AN Whitlock, 'Classification of the Law of Trusts' (1913) 1 *California Law Review* 215, 218:

> It is submitted that the *cestui* has in fact something more than a right *in personam*, that such a right might be more properly described as a right in *personam ad rem*, or, possibly, a right *in rem per personam*.

Surely such nebulous and cumbrous expressions as these could hardly fail to make 'confusion worse confounded'.

10 See Beale, 'Equitable Interests in Foreign Property (1907) 20 *Harvard Law Review* 382 and compare the important cases *Fall* v *Eastin* (1905) 75 Neb 104; (1909) 215 US 1, 14-15 (especially concurring opinion of Holmes J); *Sclover, Bates and Co* v *Walsh* (1912) 226 US 112 and *Bank of Africa Ltd* v *Cohen* [1909] 2 Ch.129, 143.

11 (1882) 20 Ch D 562, 580 per Sir George Jessel MR:

> If then the rule as to remoteness applies to a covenant of this nature, this covenant clearly is bad as extending beyond the period allowed by the rule. Whether the rule applies or not depends upon this, as it appears to me, does or does not the covenant give an interest in the land? ... If it is a mere personal contract it cannot be enforces against the assignee. Therefore the company must admit that somehow it binds the land. But if it binds the land, it creates an equitable interest in the land.

12 Compare *Ball* v *Milliken* (1910) 31 RI 36; 76 Atl 789, 793, involving a point other than perpetuities, but quoting in support of the decision reached Sir George Jessel's language as to 'equitable interests in land'. See preceding note.

13 Compa e, to the same effect, OW Holmes, *The Common Law* (1881) 409.

14 F Pollock and FW Maitland, *History of English Law*, 2nd edn (1905) 226.

15 *Ibid* 124.

[16] (1895) 67 Fed Rep 674, 677. For a somewhat similar, and even more confusing form of statement, see *In re Fixen* (1900) 102 Fed Rep 295, 296.

[17] (1872) 51 NH 504, 511. See also the excellent similar statements of Comstock J and Selden J in *Wynehamer* v *People* (1856) 13 NY 378, 396, 433-434; of Ryan C in *Law* v *Rees Printing Co* (1894) 41 Neb 127, 146 and Magruder J in *Dixon* v *People* (1897) 168 Ill 179, 190.

Compare the remarks by Gray J, dissenting, in *Roberson* v *Rochester Folding Box Co* (1902) 171 NY 538, 64 NE 442:

> Property is not, necessarily, the thing itself, which is owned; it is the right of the owner in relation to it. The right to be protected in one's possession of a thing, or in one's privileges to it. The right to be protected in one's possession of a thing, or in one's privileges, belonging to him as an individual, or secured to him as a member of the commonwealth, is property, and as such entitled to the protection of the law.

[18] (1893) 116 Mo 527, 533-534. That the last sentence quoted is not altogether adequate, as an analysis of property will appear, it is hoped, from the latter part of the present discussion. See also, as regards the term, 'property,' the opinion of Doe CJ in *Smith* v *Fairloh* (1894) 68 NH 123, 144-145: 'By considering the property dissolved into the legal rights of which it consists,' etc.

[19] W Blackstone, *Commentaries* (1765) bk 2, 16-43.

[20] Compare F Pollock and FW Maitland, *History of English Law*, 2nd edn (1905) vol. 2, 31:

> Few, if any, of the terms in our legal vocabulary have always been technical terms. The license that the man of science can allow himself of coining new words is one by which the nature of the case is denied to lawyers. They have to take their terms out of the popular speech; gradually the words so taken are defined; sometimes a word continues to have both a technical meaning for lawyers and a different and vaguer meaning for laymen; sometimes the word that lawyers have adopted is abandoned by the laity.

Compare also *ibid* 33. Compare also the discussion of Lord Kinnear in *Bank of Scotland* v *Macleod* [1914] AC 311, 324.

[21] Hand J in *Hotchkiss* v *National City Bank* (1911) 200 Fed 287: 'A contract is an obligation attached by the mere force of law to certain acts of the parties, usually words, which ordinarily accompany and represent known intent'. Compare also Baldwin J in *McCracken* v *Howard* (1844) 2 How 608, 612.

[22] (1867) 37 Ga 124, 128 and 143 per Harris J.

[23] Compare Waldo CJ in *White* v *Multonomah Co* (1886) 13 Ore 317, 323:

> A 'right' has been defined by Mr Justice Holmes to be the legal consequence which attaches to certain facts (*The Common Law* (1881) 214). Every fact which forms one of the group of facts of which the right is the legal consequence appertains to the substance of the right.

The present writer's choice of the term 'operative' has been suggested by the following passage from JB Thayer, *Preliminary Treatise on Evidence* (1898) 393:

> Another discrimination to be observed is that between documents which constitute a contract, fact, or transaction, and those which merely certify and evidence something outside of themselves, - a something valid and operative, independent of the writing.

Compare also TE Holland, *Jurisprudence*, 10th edn (1906) 151:

> A fact giving rise to a right has long been described as a 'title'; but no such well-worn equivalent can be found for a fact through which a right is transferred, or for one by which a right is extinguished. A new nomenclature was accordingly invented by Bentham, which is convenient for scientific use, although it has not found its way into ordinary language. He describes this whole class of facts as 'dispositive'; distinguishing as 'Investitive' those by means of which a right comes into existence, as 'Divestitive' those through which it terminates, and as 'Translative' those through which it passes from one person to another.

The word 'ultimate,' sometimes used in this connection, does not seem to be so pointed and useful a term as either 'operative' or 'constitutive'.

24 Compare, however, *Illinois Steel Co* v *Ostrowski* (1902) 194 Ill 376, 384, correctly sustaining a declaration alleging the operative facts specifically instead of generically, as required by the more approved forms of pleading. See also the discussion in *Nagel* v *United Rys Co* (1913) 169 M App 284; 152 SW 621; *Erdman* v *United Rys Co* (1913) 173 Mo App 98; 155 SW 1981; *Israel* v *United Rys Co* (1913) 172 Mo App 656; 155 SW 1902.

The rules of pleading determining whether allegations must be generic or specific - and if the latter, to what degree - are, like other rules of law, based on considerations of policy and convenience. Thus the facts constituting fraud are frequently required to be alleged in comparatively specific form; and similarly as regards cruelty in a suit for divorce based on that ground. The reasons of policy are obvious in each case.

For a valuable explanation as regards specific pleading of fraud, see *Mair* v *Rio Grande Rubber Estates, Lim* [1913] AC 853, 863, 864.

25 Compare *McCaughey* v *Schuette* (1897) 117 Cal 223. While the decision in this case can be supported, the statement that the specific facts pleaded were 'evidentiary' seems inaccurate and misleading.

There are, of course, genuine instances of the fatally erroneous pleading of strictly evidential facts instead of either generic or specific operative facts. See *Rogers* v *Milwaukee* (1861) 13 Wis 610 and contrast *Illinois Steel Co* v *Ostrowski* (1902) 194 Ill 376.

26 Both operative and evidential facts must, under the law, be ascertained in some one or more of four possible modes: 1. By judicial admissions (what is not disputed); 2. By judicial notice (what is known or easily knowable); 3. By judicial perception (what is ascertained directly through the senses; cf. 'real evidence'); 4. By judicial reference (what is ascertained by reasoning from facts already ascertained by one or more of the four methods here outlined).

27 As an example of this, compare Lord Westbury in *Bell* v *Kennedy* (1868) LR 1 HL (Sc) 307: 'Domicile, therefore, is an idea of the law. It is the relation which the law creates between an individual and a particular locality or country'.

Compare the confusion in the discussion of the same subject by Farwell J in *In re Johnson* [1903] 1 Ch 821, 824-825.

Contrast the far more accurate language of Chief Justice Shaw in *Abington* v *Bridgewater* (1840) 23 Pick. 170: 'The fact of domicile is often one of the highest importance to a person; it determines his civil and political rights and privileges, duties and obligations'.

28 In this connection, the words of one of the great masters of the common law are significant. In his notable *Preliminary Treatise on Evidence* (1898) 190, Professor James Bradley Thayer said:

> As our law develops it becomes more and more important to give definiteness to its phraseology; discriminations multiply, new situations and complications of fact arise, and the old outfit of ideas, discriminations, and phrases has to be carefully revised. Law is not so unlike all other subjects of human contemplation that clearness of thought will not help us powerfully in grasping it. If terms in common legal use are used exactly, it is well to know it; if they are used inexactly, it is well to know that, and to remark just how they are used'.

Perhaps the most characteristic feature of this author's great constructive contribution to the law of evidence is his constant insistence on the need for clarifying our legal terminology, and making careful 'discriminations' between conceptions and terms that are constantly being treated as if they were one and the same. See e.g. *ibid* vii, 183, 1890190, 278, 306, 351, 355, 390-393. How great the influence of those discriminations has been is well known to all students of the law of evidence.

The comparatively recent remarks of Professor John Chipman Gray, in his *Nature and Sources of the Law* (1909) viii, are also to the point:

> The student of Jurisprudence is at times troubled by the thought that he is dealing not with things, but with words, that he is busy with the shape and size of counters in a game of logomachy, but when he fully realizes how these words have been passed and are still being passed as money, not only by fools and on fools, but by and on some of the acutest minds, he feels that there is work worthy of being done, if only it can be done worthily'.

No less significant and suggestive is the recent and characteristic utterance of one of the greatest jurists of our time, Mr Justice Holmes. In *Hyde* v *United States* (1911) 225 US 347, 391, the learned judge very aptly remarked: 'It is one of the misfortunes of the law that ideas become encysted in phrases and thereafter for a long time cease to provoke further analysis'.

See also Field J in *Morgan* v *Louisiana* (1876) 93 US 217, 223 and Peckham J in *Phoenix Ins Co* v *Tennessee* (1895) 161 US 174, 177, 178.

'Every student of logic knows, but seldom realizes, the power and the actual historic influence of terms in moulding thought and in affecting the result of controversy'. Professor

John Henry Wigmore in 'The Terminology of Legal Science (With a Plea for the Science of Nomo-thetics)' (1914) 28 *Harvard Law Review* 1. See also Beck J in *City of Dubuque* v *Ill Central R R. Co* (1874) 39 Ia 56, 64.

29 (1852) 7 How Pr 124, 130.

30 (1893) 54 Fed Rep 338, 348.

31 (1871) 3 Heisk (Tenn) 287, 306-307.
See also, for similar judicial observations: *Atchison and Neb R. Co* v *Baty* (1877) 6 Neb 37, 40: 'The term right in civil society is defined to mean that which a man is entitled to have, or to do, or to receive from others within the limits prescribed by law'; *San Francisco* v *S.V. Water Co* (1874) 48 Cal 531: 'We are to ascertain the rights, privileges, powers, duties and obligations of the Spring Valley Water Co, by reference to the general law'. *Shaw* v *Proffit* (1910) 57 Or 192, 201; 109 Pac 584, 587 per Slater J: 'The word 'right' denotes, among other things, 'property,' 'interest,' 'power,' 'prerogative,' 'immunity,' and 'privilege,' and in law is, most frequently applied to property in its restricted sense'.

Compare also G Gilbert, *Evidence*, 4th edn (1777) 126: 'The men of one county, city, hundred, town, corporation, or parish are evidence in relation to the rights, privileges, immunities and affairs of such town, city, etc'.

32 See *Kearns* v *Cordwainers' Co* (1859) 6 CB ns 388, 409, construing The Thames Conservancy Act 1857, 20 and 21 Vict c 147, s 179: 'None of the powers by this act conferred ... shall extend to, take away, alter or abridge any right, claim, privilege, franchise, exemption, or immunity to which any owners ... of any lands ... are now by law entitled'; *Fearon* v *Mitchell* (1872) LR 7 QB 690, 695: 'The other question remains to be disposed of, as to whether the case comes within the proviso of 21 and 22 Vict, c 98, s 50 that 'no market shall be established in pursuance of this section so as to interfere with any rights, powers or privileges enjoyed within the district by any person without his consent; *California Civil Code*, sec 648a: 'Building and loan associations may be formed under this title with or without guarantee or other capital stock, with all the rights, powers, and privileges, and subject to all the restrictions and liabilities set forth in this title'.); *Tennessee Constitution* (1834) art 9, sec 7: 'The legislature shall have no power to pass any law granting to any individual or individuals, rights, privileges and immunities or exemptions, other than ...'.

See also *State* v *Conlon* (1895) 65 Conn 478, 490, 491.

33 (1894) 10 Ind App 60; 37 NE 303, 304.

34 See also *Howley Park Coal etc Co* v *L and NW Ry* [1913] AC 11, 25 per Viscount Haldane LC: 'There is an obligation [of lateral support] on the neighbor, and in that sense there is a correlative right on the part of the owner of the first piece of land' and *ibid* 27 per Lord Shaw: 'There is a reciprocal right to lateral support for their respective lands and a reciprocal obligation upon the part of each owner ... No diminution of the right on the one hand or of the obligation on the other can be effected except as the result of a plain contract'.

Compare, to similar effect, *Galveston etc Ry Co* v *Harrigan* (1903) 76 SW 452, 453 (Tex Civ App). See also JC Gray, *Nature and Sources of Law* (1909), sec 25: 'Right is correlative to duty, where there is no duty there can be no right'.

35 Stayton J in *Mellinger* v *City of Houston* (1887) 68 Tex. 45; 3 SW 249, 253: 'A right has been well defined to be a well-founded claim, and a well-founded claim means nothing more nor less than a claim recognized or secured by law'.

36 (1882-3) 8 App Cas 577, 597.

37 For merely a few out of numberless judicial instances of this loose usage, see *Pearce* v *Scotcher* (1882) LR 9 QB 162, 167; *Quinn* v *Leathem* [1901] AC 495 *passim*; *Allen* v *Flood* [1898] AC 1 *passim*; *Lindley* v *Natural Carbonic Acid Gas Co* (1910) 220 US 61, 75; *Smith* v *Cornell Univ* (1894) 45 NY Supp 640, 643; *Farnum* v *Kern Valley Bk* (1910) 107 Pac 568. For a striking instance of this blurring of ideas, see Avery J in *State* v *Austin* (1894) 114 NC 855, 862: 'An individual right is that which a person is entitled to have ore receive from others, or to do under the protection of law'. See also Channel J in *Starey* v *Graham* [1899] 1 QB 406, 411.] See also below n 76.

38 TE Holland, *Elements of Jurisprudence*, 10th edn (1906) 83.

39 *Ibid* 82.

40 Compare also *ibid* 139: 'The owner of a garden has a right to its exclusive enjoyment available against no individual more than another, but against everybody'; also 163: 'Rights to personal safety and freedom … limited … by the right of parent and guardians to chastise and keep in custody persons of a tender age'. The confusion continues throughout the discussion. See 185, 200, 316, 200 n 30.

41 See JC Gray, *Nature and Sources of Law* (1909) secs 25, 45, 184.

42 *Ibid* sec 48.

43 Other instances in Professor Gray's work may be noted. In *ibid* sec 53 he says: 'So again, a householder has the right to eject by force a trespasser from his 'castle'. That is, if sued by the trespasser for an assault, he can call upon the court to refuse the plaintiff its help. In other words, a man's legal rights include not only the power effectually to call for aid from an organized society against another, but also the power to call effectually upon the society to abstain from aiding others'. This, it is respectfully submitted, seems to confuse the householder's privilege of ejecting the trespasser (and the 'no-right' of the latter) with a complex of potential rights, privileged, powers and immunities relating to the supposed action at law.

In *ibid* sec 102 the same learned author says: 'If there is an ordinance that the town constable may kill all dogs without collars, the constable may have a legal right to kill such dogs, but the dogs are not under a legal duty to wear collars'. It would seem, however, that what the ordinance did was to create a privilege - the absence of the duty not to kill which otherwise would have existed in favor of the owner of the dog. Moreover, that appears to be the most natural connotation of the passage. The latter doesn't except very remotely, call up the idea of the constable's accompanying rights against all others that they shouldn't interfere with his actual killing of the dog.

See also *ibid* secs 145, 186.

Compare the following passage from OW Holmes, *The Common Law* (1881) 214: 'A legal right is nothing but a permission to exercișe certain natural powers, and upon certain conditions to obtain protection, restitution, or compensation by the aid of the public force'.

44 It may be noted incidentally that a statute depriving a party of privileges as such may raise serious constitutional questions under the Fourteenth Amendment. Compare e.g. *Lindley* v

Natural Carbonic Gas Co (1910) 220 US 61. See also *Rideout* v *Knox* (1889) 148 Mass 368 (holding constitutional a statute limiting a landowner's privilege of erecting 'spite-fences').

45 [1901] AC 495, 534.

46 See below 36-39

47 Compare *Allen* v *Flood* [1898] AC 1.

48 For a more accurate treatment of the conception of 'liberty' and 'right,' see the discussion by Cave J quoted below 38.

49 (1889) 23 QBD 59.

Compare the similar (inaccurate) use of the expression, 'conflicting rights,' by Holmes J in *Boston Ferrule Co* v *Hills* (1893) 159 Mass 147, 149-150.

50 Cases almost without number might be cited to exemplify similar blending of fundamental conceptions and rapid shifting in the use of terms - and that, too, even when the problems involved have been such as to invite close and careful reasoning. For a few important cases of this character, see: *Allen* v *Flood* [1898] AC 1, 16 per Hawkins J: 'I know it may be asked, 'What is the legal right of the plaintiffs which is said to have been invaded?' My answer is, that right which should never be lost sight of, and which I have already stated - the right freely to pursue their lawful calling'; *ibid* 84 per Lord Halsbury: 'To dig into one's own land under the circumstances stated requires no cause or excuse. He may act from mere caprice, but his right on his own land is absolute, so long as he does not interfere with the rights of others'; *ibid* 112 per Lord Ashbourne: 'The plaintiffs had, in my opinion, a clear right to pursue their lawful calling ... It would be, I think, an unsatisfactory state of the law that allowed the wilful invader of such a right without lawful leave or justification to escape from the consequences of his action'; *Quinn* v *Leathem* [1901] AC 495, 533: *Lindley* v *Natural Carbonic Gas Co* (1910) 220 US 61, 74; *Roberson* v *Rochester Folding Box Co* (1902) 171 NY 538, 544 per Parker CJ: 'The so-called right of privacy is, as the phrase suggests, founded upon the claim that a man has the right to pass through this world, if he will, without having his picture published' and *Wabash, St L and P R Co* v *Shacklet* (1883) 105 Ill 364, 389.

In his opinion in *Attorney General* v *Adelaide Steamship Co* [1913] AC 781, 793, Lord Parker of Waddington is guilty of the fallacy of supposing that duty is the correlative of privilege. He says:

> At common law every member of the community is entitled to carry on any trade or business as he chooses and in such manner as he thinks most desirable in his own interests, and inasmuch as every right connotes an obligation no one can lawfully interfere with another in the free exercise of his trade or business unless there exist some just cause or excuse for such interference.

In *Purdy* v *State* (1901) 43 Fla. 538, 540, the anomalous expression 'right of privilege' is employed.

51 F Mackeldey, *Handbook of the Roman Law*, tr MA Dopsie (1883) secs 196-197. The same matter is put somewhat less clearly in R Sohm, *Institutes*, 3rd edn, tr JC Ledlie (1907) 28. See also *Rector, etc., of Christ Church* v *Philadelphia* (186) 24 How 300, 301, 302.

52 According to an older usage, the term 'privilege' was frequently employed to indicate a

'franchise,' the latter being really a miscellaneous complex of special rights, privileges, powers, or immunities, etc. Thus, in an early book, *Termes de la Ley*, there is the following definition: ''Privileges' are liberties and franchises granted to an office, place, towne, or manor by the King's great charter, letters patent, or Act of Parliament, as toll, sake, socke, infangstheefe, outfangstheefe, turne, or delfe, and divers such like'.

Compare *Blades* v *Higgs* (1865) 11 HL Cas 621, 631 per Lord Westbury:

> Property *ratione privilegii* is the right by which a peculiar franchise anciently granted by the Crown, by virtue of prerogative, one may have of taking animals *ferae naturae* on the land of another; and in like manner the game when taken by virtue of the privilege becomes the absolute property of the owner of the franchise.

53 See *Humphrey* v *Pegues* (1872) 16 Wall 244, 247 per Hunt J:

> All the 'privileges' as well as powers and rights of the prior company were granted to the latter. A more important or more comprehensive privilege than a perpetual immunity from taxation can scarcely be imagined. It contains the essential idea of a peculiar benefit or advantage, of a special exemption from a burden falling upon others.

See also *Smith* v *Floyd* (1893) 140 NY 337, 342; *Lonas* v *State* (1871) 3 Heisk (Tenn) 287, 306, 307; *Territory* v *Stokes* (1881) 2 NM 161, 169, 170; *Ripley* v *Knight* (1878) 123 Mass 515, 519; *Dike* v *State* (1888) 38 Minn 306; *Re Miller* [1893] 1 QB 327.

Compare *Wisener* v *Burrell* (1911) 28 Okla 546.

54 Compare *Louisville and N R. Co* v *Gaines* (1880) 3 Fed Rep 266, 278 per Baxter, Associate J: 'Paschal says [the term 'privilege'] is a special right belonging to an individual or class; properly, an exemption from some duty'.

55 For apt use of terms 'privilege' and 'privileged' in relation to libel, see Hawkins J in *Allen* v *Flood* [1898] AC 1, 20-21.

56 As regards the general duty to testify, specific performance may usually be had under duress of potential or actual contempt proceedings; and, apart from that, failure to testify might subject the wrongdoer either to a statutory liability for a penalty in favor of the injured party litigant or, in the case of actual damage, to a common-law action on the case.

The subject of witnesses is usually thought of as a branch of the so-called adjective law, as distinguished from the so-called substantive law. But, as the writer has had occasion to emphasize on another occasion (WN Hohfeld, 'The Relations between Equity and Law' (1913) 11 *Michigan Law Review*, 537, 554, 556, 569) there seems to be no intrinsic or essential difference between those jural relations that relate to the 'substantive' law and those that relate to the 'adjective' law. This matter will be considered more fully in a later part of the discussion.

57 (1583) 9 Coke 1.

58 [1898] AC 1, 19.

59 (1896) 89 Me 359.

60 (1856) 6 E and B 47, 74. For other examples of apt use of the term in question, see *Borland* v *Boston* (1882) 132 Mass 89 ('municipal rights, privileges, powers or duties'); *Hamilton* v

Graham (1871) LR 2 HL (Sc) 167, 169 per Hatherley LC; *Jones* v *De Moss* (1911) 151 Ia 112, 117; *Kripp* v *Curtis* (1886) 71 Cal 62, 63; *Lamar* v *Booth* (1874) 50 Miss 411, 413; *Weller* v *Brown* (1911) 160 Cal 515; 117 Pac 517; *Mathews* v *People* (1903) 202 Ill 389, 401; *Abington* v *North Bridgewater* (1840) 23 Pick 170; *Huntley* v *Gaskell* [1906] AC 56, 57 ('rights, privileges and immunities') and *Aikens* v *Wisconsin* (1904) 195 US 194, 206 per Holmes J: 'No conduct has such an absolute privilege as to justify all possible schemes of which it may be a part'.

61 Compare the expression: 'freedom of speech'.

62 [1898] AC 29. For the reference to Mr Justice Cave's opinion, the present writer is indebted to Salmond's work on Jurisprudence. Citing this case and one other, *Starey* v *Graham* [1889] 1 Q.B., 406, 411, the learned author adopts and uses exclusively the term 'liberty' to indicate the opposite of 'duty,' and apparently overlooks the importance of privilege in the present connection. Curiously enough, moreover, in his separate Treatise on Torts, his discussion of the law of defamation gives no explicit intimation that privilege in relation to that subject represents merely liberty, or 'no-duty'.

Sir Frederick Pollock, in his volume on *Jurisprudence*, 2nd edn (1904) 62, seems in effect to deny that legal liberty represents any true legal relation as such. Thus, he says, *inter alia*:

> The act may be right in the popular and rudimentary sense of not being forbidden, but freedom has not the character of legal right until we consider the risk of unauthorized interference. It is the duty of all of us not to interfere with our neighbors' lawful freedom. This brings the so-called primitive rights into the sphere of legal rule and protection. Sometimes it is thought that lawful power or liberty is different from the right not to be interfered with; but for the reason just given this opinion, though plausible, does not seem correct'.

Compare also F Pollock, *Essays in Jurisprudence and Ethics* (1882) ch 1.

It is difficult to see, however, why, as between X and Y, the 'privilege + no-right' situation is not just as real a jural relation as the precisely opposite 'duty + right' relation between any two parties. Perhaps the habit of recognizing exclusively the latter as a jural relation springs more or less from the traditional tendency to think of the law as consisting of 'commands', or imperative rules. This, however, seems fallacious. A rule of law that permits is just as real as a rule of law that forbids; and, similarly, saying that the law permits a given act to X as between himself and Y predicates just as genuine a legal relation as saying that the law forbids a certain act to X as between himself and Y. That this is so seems, in some measure, to be confirmed by the fact that the first sort of act would ordinarily be pronounced 'lawful,' and the second 'unlawful'. Compare *Thomas* v *Sorrel* (1673) Vaughan, 331, 351, quoted below n 103.

63 Compare *Dow* v *Newborough* (1728) Comyns 242: 'For the use is only a liberty to take the profits, but two cannot severally take the profits of the same land, therefore there cannot be an abuse upon a use' (it should be observed that in this and the next case to be cited, along with the liberty or privilege there are associated powers and rights, etc, for instance the power to acquire a title to the things severed from the realty); *Bourne* v *Taylor* (1808) 10

East 189 per Ellenborough CJ: 'The second question is whether the replication ought to have traversed the liberty of working the mines ... The word liberty, too, implies the same thing. It imports, *ex vi termini*, that it is a privilege to be exercised over another man's estates'; *Wickham* v *Hawkes* (1840) M and W 63, 78-79; *Quinn* v *Leathem* [1901] AC 495, 534 per Lord Lindley; *Pollock* v *Farmers' Loan and Trust Co* (1895) 157 US 429, 652 per White J: 'rights and liberties'; *Mathews* v *People* (1903) 202 Ill 389, 401 per Magruder CJ: 'It is now well settled that the privilege of contracting is both a liberty, and a property right'); *Ferris* v *Frohman* (1911) 223 US 424, 432 per Hughes J: 'Gave to authors the sole liberty of printing their books'; *Allgeyer* v *Louisiana* (1897) 165 US 578, 592 per Peckham, J: 'must have the liberty to do that act' and *Aikens* v *Wisconsin* (1904) 195 US 205 per Holmes J: 'It would be impossible to hold that the liberty to combine to inflict such mischief ... was among the rights which the Fourteenth Amendment was intended to preserve'.

For legislative use of the term in question, see the Copyright Act 1709, 8 Anne c.19: 'Shall have the sole right and liberty of printing each book and books for the term of ...'.

Like the word 'privilege' (see ante, 45, n.48) the term 'liberty' is occasionally used, especially in the older books, to indicate a franchise, or complex of special rights, privileges, powers, or immunities. Thus in W Noy's *A Treatise of the Principall Grounds and Maximes of the Lawes of the Kingdome* (1641) there is this definition: 'liberty is a royal privilege in the hands of a subject'; and, similarly, W Blackstone, *Commentaries* (1765) bk 2, 37 says: 'franchise and liberty are used as synonymous terms; and their definition is, a royal privilege, or branch of the king's prerogative, subsisting in the hands of a subject'.

This definition is quoted in *S F Waterworks* v *Schottler* (1882) 62 Cal 69, 106 and *Central R and Banking Co* v *State* (1875) 54., 401, 409. Compare also *R* v *Halifax and Co* [1891] 2 QB 263.

64 Compare *Proud* v *Bates* (1865) 34 LJ ns 406: 'With full power and free liberty to sink for, win and work the same, with all liberties, privileges, etc., necessary and convenient,' etc.; *Hamilton* v *Graham* (1871) LR 2 HL (Sc) 166, 167; *Attersoll* v *Stevens* (1808) 1 Taunt 183 and *Wickham* v *Hawker* (1840) 7 M and W 63, 78-79.

65 See, for example, Lurton J in *City of Owensboro* v *Cumberland Telephone etc Co* (1913) 230 US 58, 64; 33 Sup Ct 988, 990:

> That the right conferred by the ordinance involved is something more than a mere license, is plain. A license has been generally defined as a mere personal privilege to do acts upon the land of the licensor of a temporary character, and revocable at the will of the latter unless, according to some authorities, in the meantime expenditures contemplated by the licensor when the license was given, have been made'.

66 (1896) 12 App Div 17; 42 NY Sup 607, 609. See, in accord, the oft-quoted passage from *Thomas* v *Sorrell* (1673) Vaughan 331, 351:

> A dispensation or license properly passes no interest, not alters or transfers property in anything, but only makes an action lawful, which without it had been unlawful. As a license to go beyond the seas, to hunt in a man's park, to

> come into his house, are only actions, which without license, had been unlawful.

Compare also *Taylor* v *Waters* (1817) 7 Taunt 374, 384: 'Those cases abundantly prove that a license to enjoy a beneficial privilege in land may be granted, and, notwithstanding the statute of frauds, without writing'. In this case the license (operative facts) is more or less confused with privileges (the legal relation created). See also *Heap* v *Hartley* (1889) 42 Ch D 461, 470.

[Note by Cook: See also WN Hohfeld, 'Faulty Analysis in Easement and License Cases' (1917) 27 *Yale Law Journal* 66.]

67 Compare *Remington* v *Parkins* (1873) 10 RI 550, 553 per Durfee J: 'A power is an ability to do'.

68 See *People* v *Dikeman* (1852) 7 Howard Pr 124, 130 and *Lonas* v *State* (1871) 3 Heisk (Tenn) 287, 3-6-307, quoted above 31.

See also *Mabre* v *Whittaker* (1906) 10 Wash 656, 663 per Scott J: '[Washington Laws of 1871 provided in relation to community property: 'The husband shall have the management of all the common property, but shall not have the right to sell or encumber real estate except he shall be joined in the sale or encumbrance by the wife] 'Right' in the sense used there means power'.

Compare also *St Joseph Fire and Marine Ins Co* v *Hanck* (1876) 63 Mo 112, 118.

Numberless additional instances might be given of the use of the term 'right,' where the legal quantity involved is really a power rather than a right in the sense of claim.

69 It is to be noted that abandonment would leave X himself with precisely the same sort of privileges and powers as any other person.

70 Compare *Wynehamer* v *People* (1856) 13 NY 378, 396 per Comstock J: 'I can form no notion of property which does not include the essential characteristics and attributes with which it is clothed by the laws of society ... among which are, fundamentally the right of the occupant or owner to use and enjoy (the objects) exclusively, and his absolute power to sell and dispose of them'; *Bartemeyer* v *Iowa* (1873) 18 Wall 129, 137 per Field J: 'The right of property in an article involves the power to sell and dispose of such article as well as to use and enjoy it' and *Low* v *Rees Printing Co* (1894) 41 Neb 127, 146 per Ryan CJ: 'Property, in its broad sense, is not the physical thing which may be the subject of ownership, but is the right of dominion, possession, and power of disposition which may be acquired over it'.

Since the power of alienation is frequently one of the fundamental elements of a complex legal interest (or property aggregate) it is obvious that a statute extinguishing such power may, in a given case, be unconstitutional as depriving the owner of a property without due process of law. See the cases just cited.

71 For a leading case exhibiting the nature of agency powers, especially powers 'coupled with an interest,' see *Hunt* v *Rousmanier* (1823) 8 Wheat 173, 210.

It is interesting to note that in the German Civil Code the provisions relating to power are expressed in terms of powers, e.g. sec 168: 'The expiration of the power is determined by the legal relations upon which the giving of the power is founded. The power is also revocable in the event of the continuance of the legal relation, unless something different results from the latter'.

Incidentally, it may be noticed also, that as a matter of English usage, the term 'power of attorney' has, by association of ideas, come to be used to designate the mere operative instrument creating the powers of an agent.

72 For examples of the loose and confusing employment of the term 'authority' in agency cases - and that too, in problems of the conflict of laws requiring the closest reasoning - see *Pope* v *Nickerson* (1844) 3 Story 465, 473, 476, 481, 483; *Lloyd* v *Guibert* (1854) 6 B and S 100, 117; *King* v *Sarria* (1877) 69 NY 24, 28, 30-32; *Risdon, etc Works* v *Furness* [1906] 1 KB 49.

For a criticism of these cases in relation to the present matter, see the writer's article The 'Individual Liability of Stockholders and the Conflict of Laws' (1909) 9 *Columbia Law Review* 492, 512 n 46, 521 n 71; (1910) 10 *Columbia Law Review* 520, 542-544.

73 The clear understanding and recognition of the agency as involving the creation of legal powers may be of crucial importance in many cases, especially, as already intimated, in regard to problems in the conflict of laws. Besides the cases in the preceding note, two others may be referred to: *Milliken* v *Pratt* (1878) 125 Mass 374, presenting no analysis of the agency problem, and, on the other hand, *Freeman's Appeal* (1897) 68 Conn. 533, involving a careful analysis of the agency relation by Baldwin J. Led by this analysis to reach a decision essentially opposite to that of the Massachusetts case, the learned judge said, *inter alia*:

> Such was, in effect, the act by which Mrs. Mitchell undertook to do what she had no legal capacity to do, by making her husband her agent to deliver the guaranty to the bank. He had no more power to make it operative by delivery in Chicago to one of his creditors in Illinois, than he would have had to make it operative by delivery here, had it been drawn in favor of one of his creditors in Connecticut. It is not the place of delivery that controls, but the power of delivery.

74 See *Emery* v *Clough* (1855) 63 NH 552: 'right or power of defeasance'.

75 See *Hudgens* v *Chamberlain* (1911) 161 Cal 710, 713, 715. For another instance of statutory powers, see *Capital, etc Bank.* v *Rhodes* [1903] 1 Ch. 631, 655 (powers under registry acts).

76 Though the nebulous term 'rights' is used by the courts, it is evident that powers are the actual quantities involved. Thus, in the instructive case of *Carpenter* v *Scott* (1881) 13 RI 477, 479, the court said, by Matteson J:

> Under [the conditional sale] the vendee acquires not only the right of possession and use, but the right to become the absolute owner upon complying with the terms of the contract. These are rights of which no act of the vendor can divest him, and which, in the absence of any stipulation in the contract restraining him, he can transfer by sale or mortgage. Upon performance of the conditions of the sale, the title to the property vests in the vendee, or in the event that he has sold, or mortgaged it, in his vendee, or mortgagee, without further bill of sale ... These rights constitute an actual,

> present interest in the property, which, as we have seen above, is capable of transfer by sale or mortgage.

It is interesting to notice that in the foregoing passage, the term 'right' is first used to indicate privileges of possession and use; next the term is employed primarily in the sense of legal power, though possibly there is a partial blending of this idea with that of legal claim, or, right (in the narrowest connotation); then the term (in plural form) is used for the third time so as to lump together the vendee's privileges, powers and claims.

For another case indicating in substance the true nature of the vendee's interest, see *Christensen* v *Nelson* (1901) 39 Or 473, 477, 479, indicating, in effect, that the vendee's powers as well as privileges may be transferred to another, and that a proper tender constitutes 'the equivalent of payment'.

77 See *Davis* v *Clark* (1897) 58 Kan 100; 48 Pac 563, 565; *Leiter* v *Pike* (1889) 127 Ill 287, 326; *Welstur* v *Trust Co* (1895) 145 NY 275, 283 and *Furley* v *Palmer* (1870) 20 Oh St 223, 225.

The proposition hat the grantee's power is irrevocable is subject to the qualification that it might possibly be extinguished (or modified *pro tanto*) as the result of a transaction between the grantor and one having the position of *bona fide* purchaser, or the equivalent.

It is hardly necessary to add that the courts, instead of analyzing the problem of the escrow in terms of powers, as here indicated, are accustomed to stating the question and deciding it in terms of 'delivery', 'relation back', 'performance of conditions', etc.

78 In this connection it is worthy of note that EB Sugden, in his work on *A Practical Treatise of Powers*, 8th edn (1861) 4, uses, contrary to general practice, the expression, 'power of entry for condition broken'.

79 For miscellaneous instances of powers, see the good opinions in *Bank of S Australia* v *Abrahams* (1875) LR 6 Ch 265; *Barlow* v *Ross* (1890) 24 QBD 381, 384.

80 As to 'inchoate' obligations, see *Frost* v *Knight* (1872) LR 7 Ex. 111 per Cockburn CJ. This matter will receive attention in a later part of the discussion.

81 Compare *Boston R Co* v *Bartlett* (1849) 3 Cush 225:

> Though the writing signed by the defendant was but an offer, and an offer which might be revoked, yet while it remained in force and unrevoked, it was a continuing offer, during the time limited for acceptance, and during the whole of the rest of the time it was an offer every instant; but as soon as it was accepted, it ceased to be an offer merely.

Compare also the forms of statement in CD Ashley, *Contracts* (1911) 16 *et seq*.

82 See the unusually clear statement of Holmes J in *Brauer* v *Shaw* (1897) 168 Mass 198, 200: 'By their choice and act they brought about a relation between themselves and the plaintiffs which the plaintiffs could turn into a contract by an act on their part'.]

83 CC Langdell, *Summary of Contracts*, 2nd edn (1880) sec 178. Langdell's *a priori* premises and specific conclusions have been adopted by a number of other writers on the subject. See, for example, CD Ashley, *Contracts* (1911) 25 and RL McWilliams, 'Enforcement of Option Agreements' (1913) 1 *California Law Review* 122.

84 For a recent judicial expression on the subject, see *WG Reese Co* v *House* (1912) 162 Cal 740, 745 per Sloss J:

> Where there is a consideration, the option cannot be withdrawn during the time agreed upon for its duration, while, if there be no consideration the party who has given the option may revoke it at any time before acceptance, even though the time limited has not expired ... such offer, duly accepted, constitutes a contract binding upon both parties and enforceable by either.

See, to the same effect, *Linn* v *McLean* (1885) 80 Ala 360, 364; *O'Brien* v *Boland* (1896) 166 Mass 481, 483 (sealed offer).

Most of the cases recognizing the irrevocable power of the optionee have arisen in equitable suits for specific performance' but there seems to be no reason for doubting that the same doctrine should be applied in a common law action for damages. See, in accord, *Baker* v *Shaw* (1912) 68 Wash 99, 103 (*dicta* in an action for damages).

[Note by Cook: For applications of the method of analysis here presented, see Professor Arthur L Corbin, 'Offer and Acceptance, and Some of the Resulting Legal Relations' (1917) 26 *Yale Law Journal* 169 and (also by the same writer) 'Conditions in the Law of Contracts' (1919) 28 *Yale Law Journal* 739.]

85 Secs 330-333. Compare, to the same effect, WA Keener, *Quasi-Contracts* (1893) 18.

86 (1892) 142 Ill 388, 397.

87 (1861) 16 Grat 519, 525.

88 (1885) 63 NH 552.

89 (1873) 36 Ia 224, 226.

90 Compare *Attorney General* v *Sudeley* [1896] 1 QB 354, 359 per Lord Esher: 'What is called a 'right of action' is not the power of bringing an action. Anybody can bring an action though he has no right at all' and *Kroessin* v *Keller* (1895) 60 Minn 372 per Collins J: 'The power to bring such actions'.

91 (1892) 95 Cal 317, 319.

92 We are apt to think of liability as exclusively an onerous relation of one party to another. But, in its broad technical significance, this is not necessarily do. Thus X, the owner of a watch, has the power to abandon his property - that is, to extinguish his existing rights, powers, and immunities relating thereto (not, however, his privileges, for until someone else has acquired title to the abandoned watch, X would have the same privileges as before); and correlatively to X's power of abandonment there is a liability in every other person. But such a liability instead of being onerous or unwelcome, is quite the opposite. As regards another person, M. for example, it is a liability to have created in his favor (though against his will) a privilege and a power relating to the watch, - that is, the privilege of taking possession and the power, by doing so, to vest a title in himself. See *Dougherty* v *Creary* (1866) 30 Cal 290, 298. Contrast with this agreeable form of liability the liability to have a duty created - for example, the liability of one who has made to given an option in a case where the value of the property has greatly risen.

93 See the use of 'immunity' by Moore J in *Gollnick* v *Marvin* (1911) 60 Or 312, 118 Pac 1016.

94 (1895) 161 US 174, 177.

[95] (1876) 93 US 217, 222. See, in accord, *Picard* v *Tennessee, etc R. Co* (1888) 130 US 637, 642 per Field J and *Rochester Railway Co* v *Rochester* (1906) 205 US 236, 252 per Moody, J, reviewing the many other cases on the subject.

In *International and G N Ry Co* v *State* (1899) 75 Tex 356, a different view was taken as to the alienability of an immunity from taxation. Speaking by Stayton CJ, the court said (377):

> Looking at the provisions of the Act of March 10, 1875, we think there can be no doubt that the exemption from taxation given by it, instead of being a right vesting only in appellant, is a right which inheres in the property to which it applies, and follows it into the hands of whosoever becomes the owner ... The existence of this right enhances the value of the property to which it applies. Shareholders and creditors must be presumed to have dealt with the corporation on the faith of the contract which gave the exemption, and it cannot be taken away by legislation, by dissolution of the corporation, or in any other manner not sufficient to pass title to any other property from one person to another. The right to exemption from taxation is secured by the same guaranty which secures titles to those owning lands granted under the act, and though the corporation dissolved, will continue to exist in favor of persons owning the property which the immunity applies. Lawful dissolution of a corporation will destroy all its corporate franchises or privileges vested by the act of incorporation; but if it holds rights, privileges, and franchises in the nature of property, secured by contract based on valuable considerations, these will survive the dissolution of the corporation, for the benefit of those who may have a right to or just claim upon its assets.

Compare, as regards homestead exemptions, Sloss J in *Smith* v *Bougham* (1909) 156 Cal 359, 365: 'A declaration of homestead ... attaches certain privileges and immunities to such title as may at the time be held'.

[96] See *Choate* v *Trapp* (1912) 224 US 665.

[97] See *Brearly School Ltd* v *Ward* (1911) 201 NY 358; 94 NE 1001 (an interesting decision, with three judges dissenting). The other cases on the subject are collected in *Ann Cas* 1912 B, 259.

[98] See *Brearly School Ltd* v *Ward* cited in preceding note; also *International and GN Ry Co* v *State* (1899) 75 Tex 356, quoted above n 132.

[99] Compare also *Wilson* v *Gaines* (1877) 9 Baxt (Tenn.) 546, 550-551 per Turney J:

> The use in the statutes of two only of the words of the constitution, i.e., 'rights' and 'privileges,' and the omission to employ either of the other two following in immediate succession, viz., 'immunities' and 'exemptions,' either of which would have made clear the construction claimed by complainant, evidence a purposed intention on the part of the legislature not to grant the benefit claimed by the bill.

Only very rarely is a court found seeking to draw a subtle distinction between an immunity and an exception. Thus, in a recent case, *Strahan* v *Wayne Co* (June 1913) 142 MW 678, 680 (Neb) Mr Justice Barnes said:

> It has been held by the great weight of authority that dower is not immune (from the inheritance tax) because it is dower, but because it ... belonged to her inchoately during (the husband's) life ... Strictly speaking, the widow's share should be considered as immune, rather than exempt, from an inheritance tax. It is free, rather than freed, from such tax.

100 (1677) 2 Swanst 170. In *Skelton* v *Skelton*, it will be observed, the word 'impunity' and the word 'exemption' are used as the opposite of liability to the powers of a plaintiff in an action at law.

For similar recent instances, see *Vacher and Sons Ltd* v *London Society of Compositors* [1913] AC 107, 118 per Lord Macnaghten: 'Now there is nothing absurd in the notion of an association or body enjoying immunity from actions at law' and *ibid* 125 per Lord Atkinson: 'Conferring on the trustees immunity as absolute,' etc.

Compare also *Baylies* v *Bishop of London* [1913] 1 Ch 127, 139, 140 per Hamilton LJ. Compare also the remarks of Swinfen Eady J in *Thornhill* v *Weeks* [1913] 1 Ch 438, 442. For instances of the apt use of the term 'disability' as equivalent to the negation of legal power, see *Poury* v *Hordern* [1900] 1 Ch 492, 495 and *Sheridan* v *Elden* (1862) 24 NY 281, 384.

101 The next article in the present series [Section 2 of this book] will discuss the distinctions between legal and equitable jural relations; also the contrast between rights, etc *in rem*, and rights, etc *in personam*. The supposed distinctions between substantive and adjective jural relations will also be considered, - chiefly with the purpose of showing that, so far as the intrinsic and essential nature of those relations is concerned, the distinctions commonly assumed to exist are imaginary rather than real. Finally, some attention will be given to the nature and analysis of complex legal interests, or aggregates of jural relations.

[Note by Cook: As an examination of the next section will reveal, the 'next article' deals chiefly with rights, etc *in personam*, and rights, etc *in rem*. The author's untimely death prevented the carrying out of the remainder of the plan.]

Section 2

The present discussion, while intended to be intrinsically complete so far as intelligent and convenient perusal is concerned, represents, as originally planned, a continuation of an article which appeared under the same title more than three years ago.[1] It therefore seems desirable to indicate, in very general form, the scope and purpose of the latter. The main divisions were entitled: Legal Conceptions Contrasted with Non-Legal Conceptions; Operative Facts Contrasted with One Another. The jural relations analyzed and discussed under the last subtitle were, at the outset, grouped in a convenient 'scheme of opposites and correlatives';[2] and it will greatly facilitate the presentation of the matters to be hereafter considered if that scheme be reproduced at the present point:

	(right	privilege	power	immunity
Jural Opposites	(			
	(no-right	duty	disability	liability
	(right	privilege	power	immunity
Jural Correlatives	(			
	(duty	no-right	liability	disability

The great practical importance of accurate thought and precise expression as regards basic legal ideas and their embodiment in a terminology not calculated to mislead is not always fully realized - especially by the student not yet far advanced in his legal work; and it is even true that many an experienced lawyer has all too thought-lessly assumed that those matters usually considered in works on so-called 'jurisprudence' are merely 'academic' in character and devoid of substantial utility for the practitioner or judge. In order to dissipate, if possible, this fallacious notion - one so demonstrably unfortunate in its consequences as regards all departments of the law[3] - the eight conceptions represented in the above scheme were analyzed and compared in great detail, the purpose having been not only to exhibit their intrinsic meaning and scope and their relations to one another, but also to exemplify the methods, both good and bad, by which they are actually applied *in judicial reasoning* to the solution of concrete problems of litigation. The purpose last indicated must in the present discussion, as in the former one, be the justification for frequent concrete examples of judicial usage, and hence for liberal quotations from apposite judicial opinions. Instructive examples, whether by way of model or by way of warning, must also be drawn occasionally from the works of well-known legal authors.[4]

In the following pages it is proposed to begin the discussion of certain important classifications which are applicable to each of the eight individual jural conceptions represented in the above scheme. Some of such overspreading classifications consist of the following: relations *in personam* ('paucital' relations), and relations *in rem* ('multital' relations); common (or general) relations and special (or particular) relations; consensual relations and constructive relations; primary relations and secondary relations; substantive relations and adjective relations; perfect relations and imperfect relations; concurrent relations (i.e., relations concurrently legal and equitable) and exclusive relations (i.e., relations exclusively equitable).[5] As the bulk of our statute and case law becomes greater and greater, these classifications are constantly increasing in their practical importance: not only because of their intrinsic value as mental tools for the comprehending and systematizing of our complex legal materials, but also because of the fact that the opposing ideas and terms involved are at the present time, more than ever before, constituting part of the formal foundation of judicial reasoning and decision.[6] Owing to limitations of space the following pages will be confined to the first classification above indicated, viz., relations *in personam* and relations *in rem*.

The phrases *in personam* and *in rem*, in spite of the scope and the variety of the situations to which they are commonly applied, are more usually assumed by lawyers, judges, and authors to be of unvarying meaning and free of ambiguities calculated to mislead the unwary. The exact opposite is, however, true; and this has occasionally been explicitly emphasized by able judges whose warnings are worthy of notice. Thus, in *Tyler* v *Court of Registration*, Mr Chief Justice Holmes says, as regards the expression *in rem*, that 'no phrase has been more misused;' [7] and in the recent case of *Hook* v *Hoffman*, Mr Justice Franklin, in the course of a scholarly opinion involving the nature of 'proceedings *in rem,*' finds it necessary to characterize the expression '*jus in rem*' as 'somewhat obscure and ambiguous.'[8] The thoughtful judge last named is, however, kind enough to advise us of the one and only remedy for this difficulty, and prompt to attempt that remedy in his own opinion. His words are worthy of quotation:

> It is no more of a solecism to say immovable personal property than it is to say removable fixtures, nor more contradicting than in the division of actions to use the term '*in rem*,' when, under the particular state of facts, the action is primarily '*in personam*.' In the development of the law it is seldom possible, or, when possible, seldom expedient, to discard established terms. In this connection an observation by Mr Justice Holmes is peculiarly applicable: 'As long as the matter to be considered is debated in *artificial* terms, there is danger of *being led by a technical definition to apply a certain name*, and then to deduce consequences which have no relation to the grounds on which the name was applied.' (*Guy* v *Donald*, 203 U.S., 406). Instead of rejecting convenient terms because they are ambiguous or not comprehensive, it is better to explain their meanings, or, in the language of old Hobbes, 'to snuff them with distinctions and definitions,' so as to give a better light.[9]

All this being so, we are forced to recognize at the very outset that the antithetical pair of expressions, *in personam* and *in rem*, is constantly being employed as a basis for classifying at least four distinct matters; and that the respective meanings of the expression in personam and the expression *in rem* are not the same for all of the different situations involved. First, we have a fundamental classification of primary rights as rights *in personam*, and rights *in rem*; second, there is the well-known classification of all judicial proceedings into proceedings or actions *in personam* and proceedings or actions *in rem*; third, there exists the closely related classification of judgments and decrees (and the corresponding jurisdictions of courts), some being called judgments or decrees *in personam*, and the others judgments or decrees *in rem*; fourth, assuming a judgment or decree *in personam* to have been obtained as the result of what may be called the 'primary stage' of the typical judicial proceeding, the question of its so-called 'enforcement' - really the 'secondary stage' of the judicial proceeding - comes into view;[10] and such enforcement is said to be either *in personam*, as in the case of the typical contempt proceeding employed to coerce performance of a decree in equity, or *in rem*, as in the case of the typical execution sale following upon an ordinary legal judgment *in personam*.[11] Anyone who has seriously observed and reflected on the interrelation of ideas and language must realize how words tend to react upon ideas and to hinder or control them. More specifically, it is overwhelmingly clear that the danger of confusion is especially great when the same term or phrase is constantly used to express two or more distinct ideas. Professor Holland, having in mind, as regards this psychological phenomenon, a particular instance not now before us, - viz., the well-known ambiguity of the Latin *jus*, the German *Recht*, the Italian *diritto*, and the French *droit*, terms used to indicate both 'law' as such and 'a right' considered as a concrete relation created by law, - does not exaggerate in the least when he says:

> If the expression of widely different ideas by one and the same term resulted only in the necessity for these clumsy periphrases, or obviously inaccurate paraphrases, no great harm would be done; but unfortunately the *identity of terms* seems *irresistibly* to suggest an *identity between the ideas* which are expressed by them.[12]

No doubt this psychological and linguistic principle - what might be called 'the principle of linguistic contamination' - explains why certain well-known legal authors have assumed, with unfortunate effect on their reasoning and argument, that the contrasted pairs of terms *in personam* and *in rem* have the same intrinsic meaning in each of the four cases above mentioned, and therefore represent throughout a precisely similar basis of classification; also that there is some formal and symmetrical interdependence between the four classifications presented, - e.g. that primary rights *in rem* are such as may be 'enforced,' or vindicated, by proceedings and judgments *in rem*, or, similarly, that primary rights *in personam* are such as can be 'enforced.' or vindicated, only by actions or proceedings *in personam*. At a later point some of these problems and fallacies will receive incidental treatment in connection with the main thread of the discussion, and it will thus be possible to give more concrete specifications and examples. The chief purpose of the following pages is, however, to discuss, directly and exhaustively, the first of the four general classifications outlined above, i.e., rights (or claims), privileges, powers, and immunities *in personam* and rights (or claims), privileges, powers, and immunities *in rem*. Substituting what the writer ventures to suggest as equivalent and more satisfactory terms for the phrases *in personam* and *in rem*, we shall have to deal *seriatim* with eight classifications, as follows: 1. paucital rights (or claims) and multital rights (or claims); 2. paucital privileges and multital privileges; 3. paucital powers and multital powers; 4. paucital immunities and multital immunities; 5. paucital no-rights and multital no-rights; 6. paucital duties and multital duties; 7.

paucital disabilities and multital disabilities; 8. paucital liabilities and multital liabilities. Each of these eight definite classifications must, for the sake of clearness, receive somewhat separate treatment. Owing, however, to limitations of space, the present article will deal chiefly with the first subdivision, i.e., paucital rights, or claims, and multital rights, or claims.

As more fully shown in the former article, the word 'right' is used generically and indiscriminately to denote any sort of legal advantage, whether claim, privilege, power, or immunity.[13] In its narrowest sense, however, the term is used as the correlative of duty;[14] and, to convey this meaning, the synonym 'claim' seems the best.[15] In what follows, therefore, the term 'right' will be used solely in that very limited sense according to which it is the correlative of duty. It is hoped that the meaning and importance of this needful discrimination may gain in concreteness and clearness as further details and examples come into view.

It is necessary at this point to venture a preliminary explanation of the division or classification now before us - confessing at once that it represents a departure from accepted modes of statement or definition on the part of learned authors and judges. It will then remain for the more detailed discussion and argument to show, if possible, that the currently received explanations are not only essentially faulty as regards analysis but also seriously misleading for the very practical purpose of solving legal problems as swiftly and accurately as possible.

A paucital right, or claim (right *in personam*), is either a unique right residing in a person (or group of persons) and availing against a single person (or single group of persons);[16] or else it is one of a *few* fundamentally similar, yet separate, rights availing respectively against a few definite persons.[17] A multital right, or claim (right *in rem*), is always *one* of a large *class* of *fundamentally similar* yet separate rights, actual and potential,[18] residing in *a single* person (or single group of persons) but availing *respectively* against persons constituting a very large and indefinite class of people.[19]

Probably all would agree substantially on the meaning and significance of a right *in personam*, as just explained; and it is easy to give a few preliminary examples: If B owes A a thousand dollars, A has an *affirmative* right *in personam*, or paucital right, that B shall do what is necessary to transfer to A the legal ownership of that amount of money. If, to put a contrasting situation, A already has title to one thousand dollars, his rights against others in relation thereto are multital rights, or rights *in rem*. In the one case the money is *owed* to A; in the other case it is *owned* by A.[20] If

Y has contracted to work for X during the ensuing six months, X has an *affirmative* right *in personam* that Y shall render such service, as agreed. Similarly as regards all other contractual or quasi-contractual rights of this character. On the other hand, there may occasionally be rights *in personam* of a *negative* tenor or content. Thus if K, a distinguished opera singer, contracts with J that the former will not for the next three months sing at any rival opera house, J has a *negative* right *in personam* against K; and the latter is under a correlative *negative duty*. In this, as in other cases of rights in the sense of claims, the right of J is but one phase of the total relation between J and K, and the duty of K is another phase of the same relation, - that is, the whole 'right - duty' relation may be viewed from different angles.

In contrast to these examples are those relating to rights, or claims, *in rem* – i.e., multital rights. If A owns and occupies Whiteacre, not only B but also a great many other persons - not necessarily all persons[21] - are under a duty, e.g. not to enter on A's land. A's right against B is a multital right, or right *in rem*, for it is simply one of A's class of *similar*, though separate, rights, actual and potential, against *very many* persons. The same points apply as regards A's right that B shall not commit a battery on him, A's right that B shall not alienate the affections of A's wife, and A's right that B shall not manufacture a certain article as to which A has a so-called patent. Further examples of such *negative*[22] multital rights will readily occur to the reader. Numerous important instances will require detailed consideration from time to time.

In spite of the formal and abstract explanations already given, and in spite of the concrete examples added for merely preliminary purposes, the effort to give an incisive and comprehensive appreciation of the conceptual and linguistic difficulties and dangers involved in the expressions under consideration would doubtless fail, at least as regards the inexperienced student, unless considerably more were done by way of direct discussion of common errors. That is to say, it seems necessary to show very concretely and definitely how, because of the unfortunate terminology involved, the expression 'right *in rem*' is all too frequently misconceived, and meanings attributed to it that could not fail to blur and befog legal thought and argument. Some of these loose and misleading usages will now be considered in detail, it being hoped that the more learned reader will remember that this discussion, being intended for the assistance of law school students more than for any other class of persons, is made more detailed and elementary than would otherwise be necessary.

(a) A right *in rem* is not a right 'against a thing'

In *Hook* v *Hoffman*, we are told by Mr Justice Franklin, in hopeful vein, that 'the somewhat obscure and ambiguous expression "*jus in rem*", when standing by itself, catches a borrowed clearness from the expression "*jus in personam*", to which it is opposed'.[23] This is laudable optimism! It cannot, however, be shared by one who has, in the course of many years, observed not only the ways and tendencies of many hundreds of intelligent students, but also the not unnatural slips of the more learned. Any person, be he student or lawyer, unless he has contemplated the matter analytically and assiduously, or has been put on notice by books or other means, is likely, first, to translate right *in personam* as a right *against a person*; and then he is almost sure to interpret right *in rem*, naturally and symmetrically as he thinks, as a right *against* a *thing*. Assuming that the division represented by *in personam* and *in rem* is intended to be mutually exclusive, it is plausible enough to think also that if a right *in personam* is simply a right against *a person*, a right *in rem* must be a right that is *not against a person*, but *against a thing*. That is, the expression right *in personam*, standing alone, seems to encourage the impression that there must be rights that are *not* against persons. Then, of course, such a supposed, though erroneous, contrast is further encouraged by the *prima facie* literal meaning of the Latin phrase *in rem*, considered *per se*; for it cannot be assumed that the average person is acquainted with the peculiar history and special meaning of that phrase. Such a notion of rights *in rem* is, as already intimated, crude and fallacious; and it can but serve as a stumbling-block to clear thinking and exact expression. A man may indeed sustain close and beneficial *physical* relations to a given *physical thing*: he may *physically* control and use such thing, and he may *physically* exclude others from any similar control or enjoyment. But, obviously, such purely *physical* relations could as well exist quite apart from, or occasionally in spite of, the law of organized society: physical relations are wholly distinct from jural relations.[24] The latter take significance from the law; and, since the purpose of the law is to regulate the conduct of human beings, all jural relations must, in order to be clear and direct in their meaning, be predicated of such human beings.

The words of able judges may be quoted as showing their realization of the practical importance of the point now being emphasized: 1900, Mr Chief Justice Holmes, in *Tyler* v *Court of Registration*:

> All proceedings, like all rights, are really against persons. Whether they are proceedings or rights in rem depends on the number of persons affected.[25]

1905, Mr Justice Markby, *Elements of Law*:

> If we attempt to translate the phrase [*in rem*] literally, and get it into our heads that *a thing*, because rights exist *in respect of it*, becomes a sort of *juristical person*, and *liable to duties*, we shall get into *endless confusion*.[26]

What is here insisted on, i.e. that all rights *in rem* are against persons, is not to be regarded merely as a matter of taste or preference for one out of several equally possible forms of statement or definition. Logical consistency seems to demand such a conception, and nothing less than that. Some concrete examples may serve to make this plain. Suppose that A is the owner of Blackacre and X is the owner of Whiteacre. Let it be assumed, further, that, in consideration of $100 *actually paid* by A to B,[27] the latter agrees with A never to enter on X's land, Whiteacre. It is clear that A's right against B concerning Whiteacre is a right *in personam*, or paucital right; for A has no similar and separate rights concerning Whiteacre availing respectively against other persons in general. On the other hand, A's right against B concerning Blackacre is obviously a right *in rem*, or multital right; for it is but one of a very large number of fundamentally similar (though separate) rights which A has respectively against B, C, D, E, F, and a great many other persons. It must now be evident, also, that A's Blackacre right against B is, *intrinsically considered*, of the same general character as A's Whiteacre right against B. The Blackacre right differs, so to say, only *extrinsically*, that is, in having many fundamentally similar, though distinct, rights as its 'companions'. So, in general, we might say that a right *in personam* is one having few, if any, 'companions'; whereas a right *in rem* always has many such 'companions'.

If, then the Whiteacre right, being a right *in personam*, is recognized as a right against *a person*, must not the Blackacre right also, being, point for point, intrinsically of the same general nature, be conceded to be a right against a *person?* If not that, what is it? How can it be apprehended, or described, or delimited at all?

If it be said that, as regards Blackacre, A has besides his rights, or claims, against B, C, D, E, and others, various *legal privileges* of controlling and using the land, and that these exist 'to, over, or against' the land, one answer might be that as regards *Whiteacre* also A has similar *privileges* against B, C, D, E and all others excepting X, the true owner. But the really relevant and paramount reply at this point is that we are now dealing only with multital rights, or claims, and not with multital privileges. The latter will require attention in a late part of the discussion.[28] It may, however, even at this point be incidentally noticed that the general tendency to 'confuse' or 'blend' legal privileges with legal rights, or claims, has doubtless contributed greatly to the hazy conception of a right *in rem* as a right to, over, or against a thing.

For the reasons already given the following passages from legal treatises and judicial opinions seem open to question in one or more particulars: 1874, Mr Stephen Martin Leake, *Law of Property in Land*:

> Jurisprudence distinguishes Rights, *using* the term *in the strict legal meaning*, into the two classes of Rights *to Things* and Rights *against Persons*, familiarly known in the civil law by the terms *jura in rem* and *jura in personam ... Rights to things, jura in rem,* have for their *subject* some *material thing*, as land or goods, which the owner may *use* or *dispose* of in any manner he pleases within the limits prescribed by the terms of his right. A right of this kind *imports in all persons* generally *the* correlative negative *duty* of abstaining from any interference with the exercise of it by the owner; and by enforcing *this duty* the law *protects and establishes the right.* But a right of this kind *does not import any positive duty* in any *determinate person*,or require any act or intervention of such person *for its exercise and enjoyment ... Rights against persons, jura in personam*, on the other hand, have for their *subject* an *act or performance* of some certain determinate person, as the payment of money, the delivery of goods and the like. A right of this kind imports the correlative *positive* legal duty in the determinate person to act in the manner prescribed. It *depends for its exercise or enjoyment* upon the performance of that duty, and is secured by the legal remedies provided for a breach of performance ... *Rights to things, jura in rem*, vary and are distinguished according to the *things or material subjects* in the use or disposal of which the right consists.'[29]

The learned author, whose book is well known to law students and highly valued for its general clearness and accuracy, has been unfortunate in treating '*in rem*' as if it meant '*to a thing*'; and it would seem that he was influenced to do this, partly at least, as a result of confusing legal privileges and legal rights. More than that, this first error has led to an additional one: that of conveying the impression that all rights *in rem* (multital rights), in order to be such, must relate to a *material thing*. Such a limitation would exclude not only many rights *in rem*, or multital rights, relating to *persons*, but also those constituting elements of patent interests, copyright interests, etc. Finally the learned author falls into the error of asserting that all rights *in personam* are *affirmative* in character; whereas they may occasionally be *negative*, as heretofore seen.

1916, Professor Joseph Henry Beale, *Treatise on Conflict of Laws*:

> The nature of rights. - The primary purpose of law being the creation of rights, and the chief task of the Conflict of Laws to determine the place where a right arose and the law that created it, a more careful study of the nature of rights is, of course, desirable before the examination of actual cases of conflict is begun ... Since we are fortunate enough to have different words for these ideas [law and rights] it is all the more necessary that we should fully understand each of them ... A right may be defined as a legally recognized interest in, to, or against a person or a thing.[30]

1903, Mr Herbert Thorndyke Tiffany, *Modern Law of Real Property*:

> Powers of attorney, by which one person is nominated as an agent to make a transfer or do some other act in the name and stead of the principal, are sometimes spoken of as common-law powers. Such an authority, however, while it did exist as common law, is *entirely different* from the powers here considered (ie, powers of appointment), since it is merely an agency in the person to whom the power is given, authorizing him to execute an instrument of conveyance or to do some other act in the place and stead of his principal, the title passing, not by the power of attorney, but by the conveyance subsequently made, which is regarded as made by the principal. *A power of attorney* creates merely a *contractual relation, - rights in personam,* - as does any other contract of agency; *while a power, such as we here treat* of, involving dominion over land to a greater or less extent, creates in the person to whom the power is given *rights in rem* of a proprietary character.[31]

The exact meaning of the learned author is not evident; but it seems clear that the *power* of an agent to convey Whiteacre is not intrinsically different, so long as it endures, from a power to convey Whiteacre in exercise of a so-called power of appointment. It is true that the agent is subject to a *liability* of having his power 'revoked' or divested by the principal, whereas the power of appointment is subject to no similar liability at the hands of anyone. But this difference, conceding its greater importance is, of course, not accurately expressed by asserting that the power of attorney creates rights *in personam*, 'merely a contractual relation,' and the power of appointment 'creates in the person to whom the power is given rights *in rem* of a proprietary character.' In truth the creation of a *power of agency* does not necessarily involve any contract rights against the principal or anyone else.[32] The fact seems to be that the greater 'staying' quality of the power of appointment (as compared with the power of agency) has suggested to the author greater 'adhesiveness' or 'thingness,' and hence caused the inappropriate terms now under review. Further critical consideration of the last-quoted passage will be desirable in connection with the subject of immunities *in personam* and immunities *in rem.*

1828, Sir Thomas Plumer, M.R., in *Dearle* v *Hall*:

> They say, that they were not bound to give notice to the trustees; for that notice does not form part of the necessary conveyance of an equitable interest. I admit, that, if you mean to rely on contract with the individual, you do not need to give notice; from the moment of the contract, he, with whom you are dealing, is personally bound. But if you man to go further, and to make *your right* attach *upon the thing* which is the subject of the contract, it is necessary to give notice; and, unless notice is given, you do not do that which is essential in all cases of transfer of personal property ... Notice, then, is necessary to perfect the title, - to give *a complete right in rem*, and not merely a right as against him who conveys his interest.[33]

This passage from *Dearle* v *Hall* will require further treatment in connection with the subject of immunities *in personam* and immunities *in rem.*

1857, Mr Justice Cutting, in *Redington* v *Frye*:

> But a sub-contractor has *no claim against the owner of the property* - his claim is only *against the property (in rem)*, and the person and property of his employer (*in personam*).[34]

The preceding quotations from legal treatises and judicial opinions have been presented, as is evident, for the purpose of exemplifying the less careful and exact use of terms that we sometimes find, and for the further purpose of indicating the confusion of thought that is likely to result in such cases. Over against these will now be considered various passages from legal treatises and judicial opinions exemplifying more precise modes of thought and expression. It is desirable to begin with Austin; for his work on *Jurisprudence* was the first to give prominence to the terms right *in rem* and right *in personam* among English-speaking lawyers and authors, and his language has become classical in its importance: 1832, Professor John Austin, *Lectures on Jurisprudence or The Philosophy of Positive Law*:

> The distinction between Rights which I shall presently endeavour to explain, is that all-pervading and important distinction which has been assumed by the Roman Institutional Writers as the main ground-work of their arrangement: namely, the distinction between rights *in rem* and rights *in personam*; or rights which avail against persons generally or universally, and rights which avail exclusively against certain or determinate persons[35] ... The terms '*jus in rem*' and '*jus in personam*' were devised by the Civilians of the Middle Ages, or arose in times still more recent ... The phrase *in rem* denotes the compass, and not the subject of the right. It denotes that the right in question avails against persons generally; and not that the right in question is a right over a thing. For, as I shall show hereafter, many of the rights, which are *jura* or rights *in rem*, are either rights over, or to, persons, or have no subject (person or thing) ... The phrase *in personam* is an elliptical or abridged expression for 'in personam certam sive determinatam.' Like the phrase *in rem*, it denotes the *compass* of the right. It denotes that the right avails exclusively against a determinate person, or against determinate persons.[36]

Additional explanations of ideas and terms and further instructive examples of usage are to be found in the following utterances of able judges: 1871, Mr Justice Markby, *Elements of Law*:

> The term 'right *in rem*' is a very peculiar one; translated literally it would mean nothing. The use of it in conjunction with the term '*in personam*' as the basis of a classification of actions in the Roman law has been explained above, and its meaning will be further illustrated

by two passages in the Digest of Justinian. In Book iv. tit. 2. sec. 9, the rule of law is referred to - that what is done under the influence of fear should not be binding: and commenting on this it is remarked, that the lawgiver speaks here generally and '*in rem*,' and does not specify any particular kind of persons who cause the fear; and that therefore the rule of law applies, whoever the person may be. Again, in Book xliv. tit. 4. sec. 2, it is laid down that, in what we should call a plea of fraud, it must be specially stated whose fraud is complained of, 'and not *in rem*.' On the other hand, it is pointed out that, if it is shown whose fraud is complained of, it is sufficient; and it need not be said whom the fraud was intended to injure; for (says the author of the Digest) the allegation that the transaction is void, by reason of the fraud of the person named, is made '*in rem*.' In all these three cases '*in rem*' is used as an adverb, and I think we should express as nearly as possible its exact equivalent, if we substituted for it the English word 'generally.' In the phrase 'right *in rem*' it is used as an adjective, and the equivalent English expression would be a 'general right'; but a more explicit phrase is a 'right availing against the world at large': and if this, which is the true meaning of the phrase 'right *in rem*,' be carefully remembered, no mistake need occur.[37]

1883, Mr Justice Mulkey, in Wabash, St L and P Ry Co v Shacklet:

One of *the primary rights* of the citizen, sanctioned by the positive law of the State, is security to life and limb, and indemnity against personal injuries occasioned by the negligence, fraud or violence of others. This is a right which *avails against all persons whomsoever*, and is distinguished from a right which avails against *a particular individual* or a determinate class of persons. The former is called a right *in rem*, the latter a right *in personam*. The former class of rights exists *independently of contract*; the latter frequently arises out of contract ... So in the present case, appellee's intestate had *a right in rem, or a general right*, which entitled him, if free from fault himself, to be protected and indemnified against injuries resulting from the negligence of all persons whomsoever, including the appellant.[38]

1886, Mr Justice Holmes, in *Hogan* v *Barry*:

There is no doubt that *an easement* may be created by words sounding in *covenant*. *Bronson* v *Coffin*, 108 Mass., 175, 180. If the *seeming covenant* is *for a present enjoyment* of a nature recognized by the law as capable of being conveyed and made an easement, -

capable, that is to say, of being *treated as a jus in rem*, and as not merely the subject of a *personal undertaking*, - and if the deed discloses that the covenant is for the benefit of adjoining land conveyed at the same time, the covenant must be construed as a grant, and, as is said in Plowden, 308, 'the phrase of speech amounts to the effect to vest a present property in you.' An easement will be created and attached to the land conveyed, and will pass with it to assigns, whether mentioned in the grant or not.[39]

1903, Mr Justice Holmes, in International Postal Supply Co v Bruce:

As the United States could not be made a party the suit failed. In the case at bar the United States is *not the owner* of the machines, it is true, *but it is a lessee in possession*, for a term which has not expired. It *has a property, a right in rem*, in the machines, which, though less extensive than absolute ownership, has the same incident of a right to use them while it lasts.[40]

1904, Mr Justice Holmes, in *Baltimore Shipbuilding Co* v *Baltimore*:

In the next place, as to the interest of the United States in the land. This is a mere *condition subsequent*. There is *no easement or present right in rem*. The *obligation* to keep up the dock and to allow the United States to use it carries active duties and is *purely personal* ... The United States has *no present right to the land*, but *merely a personal claim* against the corporation, reinforced by a condition.[41]

1905, Mr Justice Holmes, in *Muhlker* v *Harlem R.R. Co*:

What the plaintiff claims is *really property*, a *right in rem*. It is *called contract* merely to bring it within the contract clause of the Constitution.[42]

1913, Viscount Haldane, Lord Chancellor, in *Attenborough* v *Solomon*:

But the question which goes to the root of this case is one which renders such a proposition wholly beside the point. If I am right, there is no question here of an executor acting in the execution of his powers, so far as this residue is concerned. The executors had long ago lost their vested right of property as executors and become, so far as the title to it was concerned, trustees under the will. Executors they

> remained, but they were executors who had become divested, by their assent to the dispositions of the will, of the property which was theirs *virtute officii*; and their *right in rem*, their title of property, had been *transformed* into a *right in personam*, - a right to get the property back by proper proceedings against those in whom the property should be vested if it turned out that they required it for payment of debts for which they had made no provision.[43]

1914, Viscount Haldane, Lord Chancellor, in *Sinclair* v *Brougham*:

> The difficulty of establishing a *title in rem* in this case arises from the apparent difficulty of following money. In most cases money cannot be followed. When sovereigns or bank notes are paid over as currency, so far as the payer is concerned, they cease *ipso facto* to be the subjects of *specific title* as chattels. If a sovereign or bank note be offered in payment it is, under ordinary circumstances, no part of the duty of the person receiving it to inquire into title. The reason of this is that chattels of such a kind form part of what the law recognizes as currency, and treats as passing from hand to hand in point, no merely of possession, but of property. It would cause great inconvenience to commerce if in this class of chattel an exception were not made to the general requirement of the law as to title ... That seems to be, so far as the doctrine of the common law is concerned, the limit to which the exception to the rule about currency was carried; whether the case be that of a thief or of a fraudulent broker, or of money paid under mistake of fact, you can, even at law, follow, but only so long as the *relation of debtor and creditor* has *not superseded* the *right in rem*.[44]

1914, Lord Summer, in *Sinclair* v *Brougham*:

> Analogous cases have been decided with regard to *chattels*. They differ, no doubt, because of the fact that the property in the chattels remained unchanged, though identification and even identity of the subject-matter of the property failed, whereas here, except as to currency, and even there only in a restricted sense, *the term properly*, as we use that term of chattels, does not apply, and, at least as far as intention could do it; both depositors and shareholders had given up the right to call the money or its *proceeds their own*, and had taken instead *personal claims* on the society.[45]

1916, Mr Justice Brandeis, in *Kryger* v *Wilson*:

> If the plaintiff in error had not submitted himself to the jurisdiction of the court, the decree could have determined only the *title to the land*, and would have *left him free to assert any personal rights* he may have had under the *contract*.[46]

(b) A multital right or claim (right *in rem*), is not always one relating to a thing, i.e. a tangible object

If the preceding discussion has served its various purposes, it must now be reasonably clear that the attempt to conceive of a right *in rem* as a right *against a thing* should be abandoned as intrinsically unsound, as thoroughly discredited according to good usage, and, finally, as all too likely to confuse and mislead. It is desirable, next, to emphasize, in more specific and direct form, another important point which has already been incidentally noticed: that a right *in rem* is not necessarily one *relating to*, or *concerning*, a thing, ie, a tangible object. Such an assumption, although made by Leake and by many others who have given little or no attention to fundamental legal conceptions, is clearly erroneous. The term right *in rem* (multital right) is so generic in its denotation as to include: 1. Multital rights, or claims, relating to a definite *tangible object*: eg a landowner's right that any ordinary person shall not enter on his land, or a chattel owner's right that any ordinary person shall not physically harm the object involved, - be it horse, watch, book, etc. 2. Multital rights (or claims) relating neither to definite tangible object nor to (tangible) person, eg a patentee's right, or claim, that any ordinary person shall not manufacture articles covered by the patent; 3. Multital rights, or claims, relating to the holder's *owner person*, e.g. his right that any ordinary person shall not strike him, or that any ordinary person shall not restrain his physical liberty, i.e., 'falsely imprison' him; 4. Multital rights residing in a given person and relating to *another* person, e.g. the right of a father that his daughter shall not be seduced, or the right of a husband that harm shall not be inflicted on his wife so as to deprive him of her company and assistance; 5. Multital rights, or claims, not relating directly to either a (tangible) person or a tangible object, e.g. a person's right that another shall not publish a libel of him, or a person's right that another shall not publish his picture, - the so-called 'right of privacy' existing in some states, but not in all.

It is thus seen that some rights *in rem*, or multital rights, relate fairly directly to *physical objects*; some fairly directly to *persons*; and some fairly directly *neither to tangible objects nor to persons*.

It is, however, important to observe that there is a more specific Latin term, *jus in re*, which has been frequently used by able judges to indicate jural relations *in rem* (i.e., multital rights, privileges, powers, and immunities) directly concerning a tangible object, such as a piece of land, a vessel, etc. This form of expression appears to have been used by the classical Roman jurists almost exclusively in the more specific combination, *jus in re aliena* (easements, profits, etc.), as contrasted with *jus in re propria*; but the more generic *jus in re* was freely employed by the modern civilians, - especially in opposition to a particular kind of *jus in personam* called *jus ad rem*.[47]

The following explanations and examples of modern usage by able judges are worthy of careful and critical consideration: 1871, Mr Justice Markby, *Elements of Law*:

> It is necessary to distinguish carefully between a right *in rem* and a (so-called) real right. A *real* right is a right over a specific thing (a *jur in re*, as will be explained hereafter). Thus a right of ownership is a *real* right; it is also a right *in rem*. But a right to personal safety is not a *real* right, though it is a right *in rem*.[48]

1914, Lord Dunedin, in *Sinclair* v *Brougham*:

> The case of a *chattel* is easy: A shopkeeper delivers an article at the house of B in mistake for the house of A. An action would lie against B for restitution. Such an action could easily be founded on the *right of property*. To use the *Roman phraseology*, there would be a *jus in re*. And where there was a *jus in re* there would not be, I take it, any difficulty in finding a form of common law action to fit the situation. But the moment you come to deal with what in Roman phraseology is called a fungible, and especially when you deal with money, then the *jus in re* may *disappear*, and with it the appropriateness of such common law action. The familiar case is the paying of money by A to B under the mistaken impression in fact that a debt was due, when in truth there was no debt due. It was to fit cases of this sort that the common law evolved the action for money had and received.[49]

1914, Lord Kinnear, in *Bank of Scotland* v *Macleod*:

> But to extend Lord Westbury's phrase so as to make it cover *personal obligations* which do not affect the *real right* of the obligor seems to me altogether extravagant. It was maintained in argument that every obligation with reference to any property or fund which involves a liability to account fell within the principle. If that were so every imperfect security, however invalid as a *real right*, would be effectual as a trust.[50]

1855, Mr Justice B.R. Curtis, in *The Young Mechanic*:

> But I will first inquire what right or interest is conferred by the statute, provided it intended to create such a lien as exists by the general admiralty law upon foreign vessels ...Though the nature of admiralty liens has doubtless been long understood, it does not seem to have been described with fulness and precision, in England or this country. That is differs from what is called by the same name in the common law, is clear; for it exists independent of possession. *The Bold Buccleugh*, 22 Eng. L. & Eq. 62; *The Nestor*, 1 Sumn. 73. That it is not identical with equitable liens, is equally clear; for the latter arise out of constructive trusts, and are *neither a jus ad rem, or a jus in re;* but simply a duty, binding on the conscience of the owner of the thing, and which a Court of Equity will compel him specifically to perform. 2 Story's *Eq. Jurisp.* § 1217; *Ex parte Foster*, 2 Story, R. 145; *Clarke* v *Southwick*, 1 Curtis, 299 ... In my opinion the definition given by Pothier of an hypothecation is an accurate description of a maritime lien under our law. 'The right which a creditor has in a thing of another, which right consists in the power to cause that thing to be sold, in order to have the debt paid out of the price. This is a *right in the thing*, a *jus in re*.' *Traité de l'Hypotheque*, art. prelim. See also, Sanders's *Justinian*, page 227 ... Whether he can make the seizure himself, only to be followed by a judicial sale, or must resort to a court for both, may be important as to remedy, but does not affect his ultimate and essential right ... Though tacitly created by the law, and to be executed only by the aid of a court of justice, and resulting in a judicial sale, it is as really a property in the thing as the right of a pledgee or the lien of a bailee for work. The distinction between a *jus in re* and a *jus ad rem* was familiar to lawyers of the Middle Ages, and is said then to have first come into practical use, as the basis of the division of *rights* into *real* and *personal*. Sanders's *Intro. to Just.*, p.49. A *jus in re* is a right, or

> property in a thing, valid as against all mankind. A *jus ad rem* is a valid claim on one or more persons to do something, by force of which a *jus in re* will be acquired. Pothier, *Traité du Droit de Domaine*, ch. Pretences; Hugo, *His du Droit Rom.*, vol 1, p. 118 ... My opinion is, that the lien conferred by the local law was an existing incumbrance on the vessel, not divested or extinguished by the death or insolvency of the owner; and that, consequently, the decree of the District Court must be affirmed.[51]

1900, Mr Chief Justice Fuller, in *The Carlos F Roses*:

> The right of capture acts on the proprietary interest of the thing captured at the time of the capture and is not affected by the secret liens or private engagements of the parties. Hence the prize courts have rejected in its favor the lien of bottomry bonds, of mortgages, for supplies, and of bills of lading. The assignment of bills of lading transfers the *jus ad rem*, but not necessarily the *jus in rem*. The *jus in re* or *in rem* implies the absolute dominion, - the ownership independently of any particular relation with another person. The *jus ad rem* has for its foundation an obligation incurred by another. Sand. *Inst. Just.* Introd., xlviii; 2 Marcade, *Expl. du Code Napoleon*, 350; 2 Bouvier (Rawle's Revision), 73; *The Young Mechanic*, 2 Curtis, 404 ... Claimants did not obtain the *jus in rem*, and, according to the great weight of authority, the right of capture was superior.[52]

1870, Mr Justice Foster, in *Jacobs* v *Knapp*:

> That statute provides that 'any person who labors at cutting, hauling, or drawing wood, bark, logs, or lumber, shall have a lien thereon for his personal services, which lien shall take precedence of all other claims except liens on account of public taxes, to continue sixty days after the services are performed, and may be secured by attachment ... At the common law the lien of a mechanic, manufacturer, or other laborer '*is neither a jus ad rem nor a jus in re: that is to say, it is not a right of property in the thing itself*, or a right of action to the thing itself'; but it is a security, derived from a 'general principle of the common law, which gives to a man who has the lawful possession of a thing and has expended his money or his labor upon it, at the request of the owner, *a right to retain* it until his demand is satisfied ... A lien, as we have seen, is *a personal right*, as well as an interest which can only be created by the owner, or by his authority. If

> Fifield, by virtue of his contract with the defendants, had a lien upon the wood, the plaintiff could acquire no lien upon the property through him. The plaintiff, as a creditor of Fifield, could not attach and hold, as against the owner, at the common law, the property in which Fifield had but the qualified interest of a pledgee. *Lovett* v *Brown*, 40 N.H., 511. Neither is a lien for the price of labor performed on an article assignable. *Bradley* v *Spofford*, 23 N.H., 447 ... The statutes of liens have enlarged *the privileges* of the party who, at common law, could only as bailee avail himself of the lien, by substituting, in the enumerated cases, attachment of the property for retention of possession; but it would be quite anomalous to regard this process of attachment as applying in favor of a stranger against a party with whom the plaintiff never contracted, and who could in no proper sense be regarded as an attaching creditor.[53]

The passage from Mr Justice Foster, the last of the above quotations, seems open to comment. If at common law the lien of the mechanic, manufacturer or other laborer consists of the 'right to retain' the 'thing' in his possession or, to use mr Justice Foster's own later and more discriminating term, a 'privilege' of retaining possession, this is certainly a '*privilege*' relating to a 'thing.' More than that, such privileges are multital privileges, or privileges *in rem*, existing not only against the owner of the chattel but also against all persons in general, and correlating with no-rights in the latter. These multital privileges relate directly to the physical '*thing*'; and they are 'rights' in the very broad sense of that term. It is difficult, therefore, to see why the term *jus in re* should not be applicable. For the latter term does not seem to be confined to rights in the sense of *claims*, this being shown by the above-quoted opinion of Mr Justice Curtis, whose characterization of common-law liens is opposed to that of Mr Justice Foster. It is also clear that the lienor has, by virtue of his possession *per se*, rights *in rem* against all others that they shall not disturb that possession or harm the object possessed. These last are rights or claims literally *relating to* the thing; and, therefore, so far at least as the literal meaning of *jus in re* is concerned there seems to be no reason why the latter expression should not be applied. It is true that if the lienor were to surrender possession he would thereby *divest* himself of his privilege (against the owner) and his rights, or claims, against the owner and others; but while those relations exist they concern the thing, and that fact is obviously not negatived by the possibility of their being divested.

The passage last quoted from Mr Justice Markby and also the extracts from the opinions of Lord Kinnear and Mr Justice Curtis show that those rights *in rem* which directly relate to *things* - land, vessels, etc - instead of being called *jus in re* are occasionally denominated *'real'* - a term meaning literally, of course, 'relating to a thing.' '*Real* rights' in this sense are opposed to rights *in personam* relating to things. Thus, e.g. if A is owner of a horse, he has *jus in re* or '*real* rights'; if, on the other hand, X is under contract to transfer the ownership of a horse to A, the latter has that sort of right *in personam* which would sometimes be called *jus ad rem*, or '*personal right*.' In the restricted sense now referred to, it seems clear that real rights as a class also exclude both rights *in personam* and rights *in rem* that do no relate directly to things, or tangible objects. The following passages may be considered with advantages: 1914, Professor EC Clark, *History of Roman Law: Jurisprudence*:

> *Jura realia* and *personalia* are expressions occasionally used by modern civilians as adjectival forms for *jura in rem* and *in personam*, but only as confined to Property Law. [E.g. the translator of Mackeldey, Pr. ii. § 15. Austin (*T.* and *N.* ii. 5, pp.977, 978; St. Note on Lect. 14, p.184) identifies the pairs without the above qualification.] This at least seems to be the meaning given by Savigny to *jura realia*, if represented by the corresponding German *dingliche Rechte*. [*System*, 1, § 56, p.369. *Alle mögliche Rechte an Sachen ... fassen wir unter dem gemeinsamen Namen der dinglichen Rechte zusammen.*].[54]

1855, Mr Justice B.R. Curtis, in *The Young Mechanic*:

> The distinction between a *jus in re* and a *jus ad rem* was familiar to lawyers of the Middle Ages, and is said then to have first come into practical use, as the basis of the division of rights into *real* and *personal*. Sanders's *Intro. to Just.* p.49. A *jus ad rem* is a valid claim on one or more persons to do something, by force of which a *jus in re* will be acquired. Pothier, *Traité du Droit de Domaine*, ch. Pretences; Hugo, *His. du Droit Rom.* vol. 1, p.118.[55]

1914, Lord Kinnear, in *Bank of Scotland* v *Macleod*:

> But to extend Lord Westbury's phrase so as to make it cover *personal obligations* which do not affect the *real right* of the obligor seems to me altogether extravagant. It was maintained in argument that every obligation with reference to any property or fund which

> involves a liability to account fell within the principle. If that were so every imperfect security, however invalid as a *real right*, would be effectual as a trust.[56]

Even when restricted as above indicated, the pair of terms, 'real' and 'personal,' seems an undesirable one for English-speaking lawyers and judges because those words are already definitely appropriated to different and independent classifications and are constantly applied in connection with the latter. Thus, eg we have '*real* property' and '*personal* property'; and this classification is obviously not parallel with that of 'real rights' and 'personal rights' - both of the latter terms being applicable either to 'personal property' relations or to 'real property' relations. Then, too, the expression '*personal* rights' is especially misleading in its connotation because, literally, it tends to suggest rights concerning a *person* as the object to which the rights relate, that is, either the person who holds the rights or some other person. It is therefore most fortunate that the pair of terms, '*real* rights' and '*personal* rights,' is not at all common on judicial opinions or in legal treatises. Over against this, however, it must be recognized that courts not infrequently use a somewhat similar pair of terms, viz., the expression 'personal rights' or 'person claims' in opposition to some such expression as 'property right,' 'title to land,' 'interest in the thing,' etc.[57]

Finally, as regards this particular matter, it must be regretted that some authors, though no courts whatever, so far as has been observed, use the terms 'real rights' and 'personal rights' as exact equivalents, respectively, for all kinds of rights *in rem* (whether relating directly to things or to persons or to neither) and all kinds of rights *in personam*. It is greatly to be hoped that such an unusual and, for the English law, misleading use of terms will not become at all common.

(c) A single multital right, or claim (right *in rem*), correlates with a duty resting on one person alone, not with many duties (or one duty) resting upon all the members of a very large and indefinite class of persons

Though fairly implicated with what has been said in the 'preliminary' explanation of ideas and terms,[58] this proposition now requires more detailed consideration; for it represents a considerable departure from the explanations or analyses to be found in treatises on jurisprudence or in books on particular branches of the law. Let us first have definitely before us some typical passages: 1832, Professor John Austin, *Lectures on Jurisprudence, or the Philosophy of Positive Law*:

> All rights reside in persons, and are rights to acts or forbearances on the part of other persons ... The essentials of *a* right *in rem* are these: It resides in *a* determinate person, or in determinate persons, and *avails* against *other persons* universally or generally. Further, *the* duty with which *it* correlates, or to which *it* corresponds, is negative: that is to say, *a* duty to forbear or abstain ... *The* duty which correlates with [a right *in rem*] attaches upon persons generally.[59]

1871, Mr Justice Markby, *Elements of Law*:

> The persons to whom a *right in rem* belongs may be changed to any extent within the limits allowed by the law, but the persons upon whom *the* duty *corresponding* to a *right in rem* is imposed cannot be changed, because all persons are under that duty.[60]

1880, Professor Thomas Erskine Holland, *Elements of Jurisprudence*:

> *A* right is available either against a *definite* person or persons, *or* against of *all persons* indefinitely ... This distinction between rights has been expressed by calling a right of the definite kind a right *in personam*, of the indefinite kind a right *in rem*.[61]

1902, Mr Solicitor-General Salmond, *Jurisprudence*:

> A real right corresponds to a duty imposed on persons in general ... The indeterminate incidence of the duty which corresponds to *a* real right, renders impossible many modes of dealing with it which are of importance in the case of personal rights.[62]

1915, Professor Harlan Fiske Stone, *Law and Its Administration*:

> One may have *a* right against all members of the community indifferently. Thus one has *the* right not to have his person or his property unlawfully interfered with, and *this* right exists generally against all members of the community.[63]

1916, Professor Samuel Williston, 'Is the Right of an Assignee of a Chose in Action Legal or Equitable?':

> Though legal ownership is conceived fundamentally as *a* right good against all the world, actual instances of such ownership are often much more narrowly limited. The owner of a chattel which has been stolen from him is likely to find *his right* against *the world* considerably qualified if the thief is in a place where the principles of market overt prevail.[64]

In opposition to the ideas embodied in the passages just given,[65] it is submitted that instead of there being a single right with a single correlative duty resting on all the persons against whom the right avails, there are many separate and distinct rights, actual and potential, each one of which has a correlative duty resting upon some one person. Repeating a hypothetical case put above, let us suppose that A is the owner of Blackacre and X is the owner of Whiteacre. It may be assumed further that, in consideration of $100 *actually paid* by A to B, the latter agrees with A never to enter on X's land, Whiteacre; also that C and D, at the same time and for separate considerations, make respectively similar agreements with A. In such a case A's respective rights against B, C, and D are clearly rights *in personam*, or paucital rights. Surely no one would assert that A has only a single right against B, C, and D, with only a single or unified duty resting on the latter. A's right against B is entirely separate from the other two. B may commit a breach of *his* duty, without involving any breach of C's duty by C or any breach of D's duty by D. For, obviously, the content of each respective duty differs from each of the others. To make it otherwise C and D would have to be under a duty or duties (along with B) that *B* should not enter on X's land. Even if that were the case, there would be said to be three *separate* duties unless B, C, and D bound themselves so as to create a so-called joint obligation. In the later case alone would there be said to be a single right and a single (joint) duty. Going beyond this direct analysis of the situation, it seems clear that the three respective 'right-duty' relations of A and B, A and C, and A and D respond to every test of separateness and independence. A might, e.g. discharge B from his duty to A, thus (in equivalent terms) creating a privilege of entering as against A (not as against X, of course); yet, obviously, the respective duties of C and D would continue the same as before. So on indefinitely.

Point for point, the same considerations and tests seem applicable to A's respective rights *in rem*, or multital rights, against B, C, D, and others indefinitely, that they, respectively considered, shall not enter on Blackacre. It is not a case of one *joint* duty of the *same* content resting on all – e.g. that B should not enter on Blackacre.[66] Consistently with this view, A might, e.g. extinguish B's duty or, in other words, grant B the privilege of entering by giving 'leave and license' to do so. In such event, of course, the respective duties of C, D, E, and all others would continue to exist, precisely as before.

In order to see even more clearly that the supposed single right *in rem* correlating with 'a duty' on 'all' persons really involves as many separate and distinct 'right - duty' relations as there are persons subject to a duty, it may be worth while to reverse the situation somewhat, and consider, in anticipation of a more general treatment at a later point, the subject of duties *in rem*, or multital duties. Thus, e.g. X is under duty not to strike R, S, T, or any other ordinary member of the community. Are we to say that, as regards these many persons, X has but a single duty,[67] and that, correlatively, there is but a *single* right held by R, S, T, and all the others? Manifestly not, for each one of these persons has a distinct and independent right; and any one of such independent rights might cease to exist without in the least affecting the others. If, e.g. R threatens bodily harm to X, R's right that X shall not strike him becomes thereby extinguished, and a no-right in R substituted; or, correlatively, in such contingency, X's duty to R ceases, and X acquires a privilege of self-defense against R. But such change in no way affects the entirely distinct relations existing between X and the various other persons involved.

As regards the separateness and relativity of all 'right - duty' relations, the following judicial reasoning seems accurate and persuasive: 1908, Mr Justice Connor, in *McGhee* v *R. Co*:

> It is elementary that plaintiff had no cause of action against defendants for placing the dynamite in the shanty. He must establish some relation between *defendants* and *himself* from which *a duty to him* is imposed upon *defendants*. 'The expression 'duty' properly imports *a determinate person to whom* the obligation is owing, *as well as the one who owes* the obligation. There must be *two determinate parties* before the relationship of obligor and obligee of a duty can exist.[68]

With this passage we may well compare the instructive opinion of an eminent English judge emphasizing the distinct and relative character of each 'privilege - no-right' relation connected with a given matter, his observations being equally applicable to 'right - duty' relations: 1906, Lord Collins, M.R., in *Thomas* v *Bradbury, Agnew, & Co, Ltd.*:

> The right [privilege] of fair comment, though shared by the public, is *the right* [privilege] of *every individual* who asserts it, and is, *qua* him, *an individual right* whatever name it be called by, and comment by him which is coloured by malice cannot from his standpoint be deemed fair. He, and he only, is the person in whose motives the plaintiff in the libel action is concerned, and if he, the person sued, is proved to have allowed his view to be distorted by malice, it is quite immaterial that somebody else might without malice have written an equally damnatory criticism. The defendant, and not that other person, is the party sued.[69]

If, then, the foregoing line of reasoning be sound, the following points would seem to be reasonably clear: A right *in rem*, or multital right, correctly understood, is simply one of a large number of fundamentally similar rights residing in *one* person; and any one of such rights has as its correlative one, and only one, of a large number of general, or common, duties, - that is, fundamentally similar duties residing respectively in *many* different persons. Similarly, a duty *in rem*, or multital duty, is one of a large number of fundamentally similar duties residing in *one* person; and any one of such duties has as its correlative one of a large number of general, or common, rights, or claim, - that is, fundamentally similar rights, or claims, residing respectively in *many* different persons. It is therefore to he hoped that, instead of continuing to be used to indicate the entire multiplicity of separate and independent rights, or claims, that a person may have against many others, the term right *in rem* may gradually come to be used to represent one, and only one, of this multiplicity of distinct rights. Whatever be the fate of the concept and term, right *in rem*, in this regard, it is surely of the utmost importance that the various possible analyses and meanings involved be carefully pondered and understood; and, in the meanwhile, the term 'multital' - free as it is from any previous hazy connotations - will without question serve definitely to indicate one, and one only, of such a multiplicity of rights as is now under consideration.

(d) A multital right, or claim (right *in rem*), should not be confused with any co-existing privileges or other jural relations that the holder of the multital right or rights may have in respect to the same subject-matter

As already incidentally noticed, it is feared that the exact nature of multital rights has been greatly obscured not only by the habitual tendency to treat a multiplicity of fundamentally similar rights, or claims, as if they were only one, but also by the equally strong tendency to include under the hazy blanket-term, right *in rem*, especially in the case of tangible objects, the multiplicity of privileges and other jural relations that the holder of the multital right or rights may have.

Suppose, for example, that A is free-simple owner of Blackacre. His 'legal interest' or 'property' relating to the tangible object that we call *land* consists of a complex aggregate of rights (or claims), privileges, powers, and immunities.[70] First, A has multital legal rights, or claims, that *others*, respectively, shall *not* enter on the land, that they shall not cause physical harm to the land, etc., such others being under respective correlative legal duties. Second, A has an indefinite number of legal privileges of entering on the land, using the land, harming the land, etc., that is, within limits fixed by law on grounds of social and economic policy, he has privileges of doing on or to the land what he pleases; and correlative to all such legal privileges are the respective legal no-rights of other persons. Third, A has the legal power to alienate his legal interest to another, i.e., to extinguish his complex aggregate of jural relations and create a new and similar aggregate in the other person; also the legal power to create a life estate in another and concurrently to create a reversion in himself; also the legal power to create a privilege of entrance in any other person by giving 'leave and license'; and so on indefinitely. Correlative to all such legal powers are the legal liabilities in other persons - this meaning that the latter are subject *nolens volens* to the changes of jural relations involved in the exercise of A's powers. Fourth, A has an indefinite number of legal immunities, using the term immunity in the very specific sense of non-liability or non-subjection to a power on the part of another person. Thus A has the immunity that no ordinary person can alienate A's legal interest or aggregate of jural relations to another person; the immunity that no ordinary person can extinguish A's own privileges of using the land; the immunity that no ordinary person can extinguish A's right that another person X shall not enter on the land or, in other words, create in

X a privilege of entering on the land. Correlative to all these immunities are the respective legal disabilities of other persons in general.

In short, A has vested in himself, as regards Blackacre, multital, or *in rem*, 'right - duty' relations, multital, or *in rem*, 'privilege - no-right' relations, multital, or *in rem*, 'power - liability' relations, and multital, or *in rem*, 'immunity - disability' relations. it is important, in order to have an adequate analytical view of property, to see all these various elements in the aggregate. it is equally important, for many reasons, that the different classes of jural relations should not be loosely confused with one another. A's privileges, eg are strikingly independent of his rights or claims against any given person, and either might exist without the other. Thus A might, for $100 paid to him by B, agree in writing to keep off his own land, Blackacre. A would still have his rights or claims against B, that the latter should keep off, etc.; yet, as against B, A's own privileges of entering on Blackacre would be gone. On the other hand with regard to X's land, Whiteacre, A has, as against B, the privilege of entering thereon; but, not having possession, he has no right, or claim, that B shall not enter on Whiteacre.

Not only as a matter of accurate analysis and exposition, but also as a fact of great practical consequence and economic significance, the property owner's rights, or claims, should be sharply differentiated from his privileges. It is sometimes thought that A's rights, or claims, are created by the law for the sole purpose of guarding or protecting A's own physical user or enjoyment of the land, as if such physical user or enjoyment of the land were the only economic factor of importance. A moment's reflection, however, shows that this is a very inadequate view. Even though the land be entirely vacant and A have no intention whatever of personally using the land, his rights or claims that others shall not use it even temporarily in such ways as would not alter its physical character are, generally, of great economic significance as tending to make others compensate A in exchange for the extinguishment of his rights, or claims, or in other words, the creation of privileges of user and enjoyment. This has been emphasized by an eminent English judge:

1874, Lord Selborne, Chancellor, in *Goodson* v *Richardson*:

> It is said that the objection of the plaintiff to the laying of these pipes in his land is an unneighborly thing, and that his right is one of little or no value, and one which Parliament if it were to deal with the question, might possibly disregard. What Parliament might do, if it were to deal with the question, is, I apprehend, not a matter for our

> consideration now, as Parliament has not dealt with the question. Parliament is, no doubt, at liberty to take a higher view upon a balance struck between private rights and public interests than this Court can take. But with respect to the suggested absence of value of the land in its present situation, it is enough to say that the very fact that no interference of this kind can lawfully take place without his consent, and without a bargain with him, gives his interest in this land, even in a pecuniary point of view, precisely the value which that power of veto upon its use creates, when such use is to any other person desirable and an object sought to be obtained.[71]

Even so able and cautious a thinker as Austin seems to have confused legal privileges with legal rights (in the sense of claims), and also, at times, to have confused mere *physical* power and liberty both with legal privileges and with legal rights. Probably because of the very failure to make these necessary and important discriminations, he appears to have overlooked, or at least seriously underrated, the practical and economic significance of the landowner's 'right - duty' relations considered wholly apart from their being guardians of the 'privilege - no-right' relations, or protectors of the *physical* liberty and power involved in the exercise of such legal privileges: 1832, Professor John Austin, *Lectures on Jurisprudence, or the Philosophy of Positive Law*:

> Now the ends or purposes of different rights are extremely various. The end of the rights *in rem* which are conferred over things, is this: that the entitled party may deal with, or dispose of, the thing in question in such or such a manner and to such or such an extent. In order to that end, other persons generally are laid under duties to forbear or abstain from acts which would defeat or thwart it ... As I stated in my last lecture, I mean by property or dominion (taken with the sense wherein I use the term, for the present) any such right *in rem* (of limited or unlimited duration) as gives to the party in whom it resides an indefinite power or liberty of using or dealing with the subject: A power or liberty of using or dealing with the subject which is not capable of exact circumscription or definition; which is merely limited, generally and indefinitely, by the sum of the duties (relative and absolute) incumbent on the owner or proprietor ... The power of user and the power of exclusion are equally rights to forbearances on the part of other persons generally. By virtue of the right or power of indefinitely using the subject, other persons generally are bound to forbear from disturbing the owner in acts of user. By virtue of the

> right or power of excluding other persons generally, other persons generally are bound to forbear from using or meddling with the subject. The rights of user and exclusion are so blended, that an offence against the one is commonly an offence against the other. I can hardly prevent you from ploughing your field, or from raising a building upon it, without committing, at the same time, a trespass. And an attempt on my part to use the subject (as an attempt, for example, to fish in your pond) is an interference with your right of user as well as with your right of exclusion. But an offence against one of these rights is not of necessity an offence against the other. If, for example, I walk across your field, in order to shorten my way to a given point, I may not in the least injure you in respect of your right of user, although I violate your right of exclusion. Violations of the right of exclusion (when perfectly harmless in themselves) are treated as injuries or offences by reason of their *probable effect* on the rights of user and exclusion. A harmless violation of the right of exclusion, if it passed with perfect impunity, *might lead*, by force of the example, to *such numerous violations of the right* as would render *both rights nearly nugatory.*[72]

In these various passages, and especially in the last one, Austin uses the term 'right' indiscriminately and confusedly to indicate both those jural relations that are legal rights, or claims, and those that are legal privileges - a lapse all the more surprising in view of the fact that the learned and painstaking author had previously been careful to emphasize the proposition that 'the term 'right' and the term 'relative duty' signify the same notion considered from different aspects.'[73] Such a delimitation of 'right' clearly excludes 'legal privilege'; for the correlative of the latter, or 'the same notion' from a 'different aspect,' is, of course, 'no-right' or 'no-claim.'

More or less similar blending of legal concepts and terms in connection with the subject of rights *in rem* seems to find place not only in well-known works on jurisprudence but also in various treatises or monographs on particular branches of the law.[74] Indeed it is not unlikely that the later writers have in this respect but followed the lead of Austin, as they have in so many other matters of legal analysis.

The following passages will serve to show how general is the usage referred to, and, it is believed, will also indicate how such a usage tends to hinder and obscure correct analysis and clear understanding of legal problems: 1871, Mr Justice Markby, *Elements of Law*:

> Thus in the case of a contract between A and B, the right of A to demand performance of the contract exists against B only; whereas in the case of ownership, the right to hold and enjoy the property exists against persons generally. This distinction between rights is marked by the use of terms derived from the Latin: the former are called rights *in personam*; the latter are called rights *in rem*.[75]

1880, Professor Thomas Erskine Holland, *Elements of Jurisprudence*:

> A right is available either against a definite person or persons, or against all persons indefinitely. A servant, for instance, has a right to his wages for the work he has done, available against a definite individual, his master; while the owner of a garden has a right to its exclusive enjoyment available against no one individual more than anther, but against everybody.[76]

1902, Mr Solicitor-General Salmond, *Jurisprudence*:

> My right to the peaceable occupation of my farm is a real right, for all the world is under a duty towards me not to interfere with it ... I have a real right to the use and occupation of my own house; I have a personal right to receive accommodation at an inn.[77]

1874, Mr Stephen Martin Leake, *Law of Property in Land*:

> Rights to things, *jura in rem*, have for their subject some material thing, as land or goods, which the owner may use or dispose of in any manner he pleases within the limits prescribed by the terms of his right. A right of this kind imports in all persons generally the correlative negative duty of abstaining from any interference with the exercise of it by the owner; and by enforcing this duty the law protects and establishes the right. But a right of this kind does not import any positive duty in any determinate person, or require any act or intervention of such person for its exercise and enjoyment.[78]

1887, Professor James Barr Ames, 'Purchase for Value without Notice':

> The most striking difference between property in a thing and property in an obligation is in the mode of enjoyment. The owner of a house or a horse enjoys the fruits of ownership without the aid of

> any other person. The only way in which the owner of an obligation can realize his ownership is by compelling its performance by the obligor. Hence, in the one case, the owner is said to have a right *in rem*, and, in the other, a right *in personam*.[79]

1915, Professor Harlan Fiske Stone, *Law and its Administration*:

> It will be noted that the *essential difference* between a right *in rem* and a right *in personam* is that a right *in rem* may be enjoyed by the possessor of it without the intervention or aid of any other person, whereas the possessor of a right *in personam* can enjoy his possession or ownership of it only by compelling the obligor to perform the obligation which gives rise to the right ... Rights *in rem* include generally all of those rights commonly spoken of as property rights; that is to say, rights to possess, use, and enjoy things, which rights are good and enforceable against all the world.'[80]

1916, Professor Samuel Williston, 'Is the Right of an Assignee of a Chose in Action Legal or Equitable?':

> Though *legal ownership* is conceived fundamentally as a right good against all the world, actual instances of such ownership are often much more narrowly limited.[81]

(e) A multital primary right, or claim (right *in rem*), should, regarding its character as such, be carefully differentiated from the paucital secondary right, or claim (right *in personam*), arising from a violation of the former

Using again the hypothetical case involving A as owner of Blackacre, it is clear that if B commits a destructive trespass on A's land, there arises at that moment a new right, or claim, in favor of A, - i.e., a so-called secondary right that B shall pay him a sum of money as damages; and of course B comes simultaneously under a correlative duty. Similarly if C commits a battery on A, or if D alienates the affections of A's wife; and so on indefinitely. In each of these cases the secondary right – e.g. that against B - is a paucital right, or claim, ie, a right *in personam*. The entire 'right - duty' relation would be one of the class of relations *in personam* designated in Roman law by the term *obligatio*. More specifically, the relation would be known as an *obligatio ex delicto*. This is brought out by the language of an eminent judge: 1904, Mr Justice Holmes, in *Slater* v *Mexican National R.R. Co*:

> We assume for the moment that it was sufficiently alleged and proved that the killing of Slater was a negligent crime within the definition of Article 11 of the Penal Code, and, therefore, if the above sections were the only law bearing on the matter, that they *created a civil liability to make reparation* to any one whose rights were infringed ... The theory of the foreign suit is that ... the act complained of ... gave rise to an obligation, an *obligatio*.[82]

This analysis seems applicable even in the case of a tort consisting of wrongfully dispossessing an owner of a tangible movable object. Thus, if Y wrongfully takes possession and control of X's horse, there arises a duty in Y to return the animal to X; and, of course, X gets a correlative right. The latter is a paucital right, or right *in personam*; for there are no fundamentally similar rights against persons in general. This is true even though, of course, X's rights against others that they shall not convert or harm the horse while in Y's possession are rights *in rem*. The following passage is apposite: 1900, Mr Chief Justice Holmes, in *Tyler* v *Court of Registration*:

> But it is said that this is not a proceeding *in rem*. It is certain that no *phrase* has been *more misused*. In the past it has had little more significance than that *the right* alleged to have *been violated* was a *right in rem*. Austin thinks it necessary to quote Leibnitz for the sufficiently obvious remark that *every right to restitution* is a *right in personam*.[83]

That this distinction is not always carefully observed may be seen from a consideration of the quotations next to be presented.

(f) A multital primary right, or claim (right *in rem*), should not, regarding its character as such, be confused with, or thought dependent on, the character of the proceedings by which it (and the secondary right arising from its violation) may be vindicated

Owing to limitations of space this matter cannot be given here all the attention that it deserves; and the more complete discussion must be reserved for another place. Some of the more important points should, however, be noticed in the present context.

At least two tendencies are occasionally to be observed by way of confusing the nature of primary rights (as *in personam* or *in rem*) with the character of the proceedings by which they may be vindicated. Both of these tendencies are believed to be founded on seriously erroneous notions that ought, if possible, to be dissipated. Each of them will, therefore, be briefly discussed.

First, it is sometimes supposed that to have a right *in rem* concerning a tangible object of which the owner has been wrongfully dispossessed means that he may recover possession of the object itself, by self-help or action, from the first wrongdoer or any subsequent party holding possession as vendee or bailee of the first wrongdoer, or as wrongful taker from the latter, Thus: 1890, Professor James Barr Ames, 'Disseisin of Chattels':

> Trespass, however, was a purely personal action; it sounded only in damages. The wrongful taking of chattels was, therefore, a more effectual disseisin than the ouster from land. The dispossessed owner of land, as we have seen, could always recover possession by an action. Though deprived of the *res, he* still had a right *in rem*. The disseisor acquired only a defeasible estate. One whose chattel had been taken from him, on the other hand, having no means of recovering it by action, not only lost the *res*, but had no right *in rem*. The disseisor *gained* by his tort both the possession and the right of possession; in a word, the *absolute property* in the chattel taken ... Today, as everyone knows, neither a trespasser, nor one taking or buying from him, nor the vendee of a bailee, either with or without delivery by the latter, acquires the absolute property in the chattel taken or bailed. The disseisee of goods, as well as the disseisee of land, has a right *in rem*. The process by which the *right in personam* has been *transformed* into a *real right* may be traced in the expansion of the writs of replevin and detinue, and is sufficiently curious to warrant a sight digression ... The disseisee's right *in rem*, however, was still *a qualified right*; for replevin was never allowed in England against a vendee or bailee of a trespasser, nor against a second trespasser. it was only by the later extension of the action of detinue that a disseisee finally acquired a *perfect* right *in rem*. Detinue, although its object was the recovery of a specific chattel, was originally an action *ex contractu*. It was allowed only against a bailee or against a vendor, who after the sale and before delivery was in much the same position as a bailee ... So long as the adverse

> possession continues, the dispossessed owner of the chattel has, manifestly, no power of present enjoyment. Has he lost also the power of alienation? *His right in rem, if analyzed, means a right to recover possession by recaption or action.*[84]

As indicated by the passages quoted, Professor Ames seems to have thought that for the owner, after dispossession, to have rights *in rem* would require the remedy of specific recovery of the tangible object. This, however, seems to involve a blending or confusing of substantive relations and adjective relations. If A, the owner of a tangible movable object, is dispossessed by B, A, under modern authorities, has rights against all persons that the object should not be harmed or 'converted'; and these rights could be vindicated by an action on the case or by an action of trover, as the facts might demand. It is clear, moreover, that such rights would exist, as multital rights, or rights *in rem*, even though no possessory remedy were open to A.

If we may judge by the passages quoted above, it seems not unlikely that Professor Ames, because of assuming that a right *in rem* concerning physical objects involves necessarily, in case of dispossession, the remedy of recovery of possession, would apparently have asserted that in the early days even a chattel owner in actual possession did not have '*a* right *in rem*';[85] and it is clear, in any event, that the possibility of regaining possession by action or self-help is frequently assumed to be of the essence of 'a right *in rem*.'

This, however, seems a very inadequate and inexact view. Even in the days when wrongful dispossession operated virtually to divest the legal interest of the chattel owner, it was still true that *prior* to any such dispossessing of the physical object and concomitant divesting of the legal interest he had rights *in rem* against persons in general that they should not harm the object or take the object from the owner; and these respective multital rights, or rights *in rem*, could, as Professor Ames himself points out, be vindicated by trespass or other action brought to secure damages.[86] In other words, the chattel owner's rights, so long as he had them, were rights *in rem*, even though in the early period now referred to (middle of the thirteenth century) he was subject to the *liabilities* of their being virtually divested by a wrongful taking, - there being, correlatively, a power in the wrongdoer thus to divest the interest of the chattel owner.[87]

Fundamentally similar legal powers and correlative liabilities involving the divesting of 'legal'[88] and 'equitable' rights *in rem* (and other jural relations belonging to the particular aggregates involved) have existed from the earliest times. Such powers are created by the law on various grounds of policy and convenience, - the teleology underlying each particular instance not being difficult to discover. In this place a bare enumeration of some of such powers must suffice: 1. The power of sale in market overt to a *bona fide* purchaser; 2. The power of even a thief having possession of money but not, of course, the 'ownership' thereof, to create a good title in a *bona fide* 'purchaser,'[89] - the whole country being in this case, so to say, 'market overt' because of the necessity of free circulation of money,m and it being too inconvenient for the transferor to produce or the transferee to examine an 'abstract of title'; 3. The power or powers of a grantor and second grantee of realty, under the recording acts, to extinguish the interest of the first grantee by a conveyance to the second grantee as an innocent purchaser and the prior recording of the latter's deed;[90] 4. The statutory power of a factor, in certain cases, to create a good title in an innocent purchaser; 5. The power of a duly appointed agent, in certain cases, to sell chattels to an innocent purchaser, even after his *factual* authorization to sell has been revoked by the principal; 6. The power of a trustee to convey an unincumbered 'legal title' to a *bona fide* purchaser for value without notice, - the equitable rights, privileges, etc., of the *cestui que trust* being thereby extinguished.

The foregoing and others that might be mentioned are cases depending on the public policy of securing freedom of alienation and circulation of property in the business world. There may now be mentioned certain other cases dependent on somewhat different teleological considerations: 1. The power of an ordinary agent (while his *factual* authorization continues) to divest the rights *in rem*, etc., in the agent's transferee; 2. The power of a donee of a power of appointment to extinguish the rights *in rem*, etc., of the owner of a vested interest and to create new and corresponding rights, etc., in the transferee; 3. The power of the appropriate officer or officers to alienate property effectually in eminent domain proceedings; 4. The power of a sheriff duly empowered by writ of execution to divest the rights *in rem*, etc., of the present owner of property and to vest new and corresponding rights, etc., in another; 5. The power of a court, in a statutory proceeding to quiet title, to extinguish the rights *in rem*, etc., of the present owner and to give new and corresponding rights, etc., to the plaintiff; 6. Various other powers of courts involving the 'shifting' of title from one person to another.

In all these cases it is clear that the present owner has rights *in rem*, etc., in spite of his *liabilities* that they may be divested through the exercise of the various powers indicated.

Second, we must now consider a second form of the same general tendency to assume some rigid interdependence between the nature of a right in rem as such and the character of the proceedings available for its vindication. This erroneous assumption has most often been made in discussions of the question whether there are any instances of equitable rights *in rem* (multital rights), or, indeed, whether there could, in the very nature of things, be any instances of equitable rights *in rem*. Thus: 1877, Professor CC Langdell, *Summary of Equity Pleading*:

> The reason why all equitable rights to property are lost the moment the legal ownership is transferred for value to a person who has no notice that it is subject to any equitable rights, will be found in the fundamental nature of *equitable jurisdiction*, as explained in previous paragraphs. It is only by a figure of speech that a person who has not the legal title to property can be said to be the equitable owner of it. What is called equitable ownership or equitable title or an equitable estate is *in truth only a personal claim* against the real owner; *for equity has no jurisdiction in rem*, and cannot, *therefore*, confer a true ownership, except by its owner over the person with whom the ownership resides, ie, by compelling him to convey.[91]

1900, Professor CC Langdell, 'Classification of Rights and Wrongs':

> Can equity then create such rights as it finds to be necessary for the purposes of justice? *As equity wields only physical power*, it seems to be *impossible* that it should actually *create anything*. It seems, moreover, to be impossible that there should be any other actual rights than such as are created by the State, ie, legal rights. So, too, if equity could create actual rights, the existence of rights so created would have to be recognized by every court of justice within the State; and yet no other court than a court of equity will admit the existence of any right created by equity. *It seems, therefore, that equitable rights exist only in contemplation of equity*, ie, that they *are a fiction* invented by equity for the promotion of justice. Still, as in contemplation of equity such rights do exist, equity must reason upon them and deal with them as if they had an actual existence.[92]

Circa 1886, Professor James Barr Ames, *Lectures on Legal History*:

> A trust, as every one knows, has been enforceable for centuries against any holder of the title except a purchaser for value without

> notice. But this exception shows that the *cestui que trust*, unlike the bailor, has not acquired a right *in rem.*[93] This *distinction* is, of course, *due* to the *fundamental difference* between *common-law* and *equity procedure*. The *common law acts in rem*. The judgment in detinue is, accordingly, that the plaintiff recover the chattel, or its value.[94] Conceivably the common-law judges might have refused to allow the bailor to cover in detinue against a *bona fide* purchaser, as they did refuse it against a purchaser in market overt. But this would have involved a weighing of ethical considerations altogether foreign to the medieval mode of thought. Practically there was no middle ground between restricting the bailor to an action against his bailee, and giving him a right against any possessor. Equity, on the other hand, *acts only in personam*, never decreeing that a plaintiff recover a *res*, but that the defendant surrender what in justice he cannot keep.[95]

1904, Professor Federick William Maitland, 'Trust and Corporation':

> I think it is better and safer to say with a great American teacher that 'Equity *could not* create rights *in rem* if it would, and would not if it could.' See Langdell, Harvard Law Review, Vol. I, p.60.[96]

It is difficult to find solid foundation for such assumptions as the foregoing, or to understand how the notions connected therewith could have received such a large following. Are we forced to recognize that mere words - especially if they are Latin words - have such a surprisingly potent tendency to control thought?

Suppose, once again, that A is owner of Blackacre, and that B drives his automobile over A's lawn and shrubbery. A's primary right *in rem* is thereby violated, and a secondary right *in personam* arises in favor of A and against B, - an '*obligatio*,' to use the term of Mr Justice Holmes.[97] A may sue B at law for damages and get, as a result of the 'primary stage' of the proceeding, an ordinary legal judgment *in personam* for (say) $500. Such judgment would 'merge' or extinguish A's secondary right *in personam* together with B's secondary duty, and would create a (new) judgment obligation - right *in personam* and correlative duty - for the payment of $500. Such judgment would be binding even though the judgment debtor, B, had no assets whatever.[98] Thus, if B's judgment duty is not performed or discharged, a new action can, in most jurisdictions, be based thereon; though in some of the latter costs are denied to the plaintiff if the new action be brought without special reasons.[99]

But of course A is not likely to wish merely an indefinite series of judgment obligations. If, therefore, B has property either at the time judgment is rendered or at some later time, a 'secondary stage'[100] of the proceedings, beginning with a writ of execution, may be had. That is, the sheriff, under such a writ, has the power and duty of selling sufficient property of B and applying the proceeds to the satisfaction of the judgment. If the total proceedings culminate in this way, and only if they do so culminate, can we say that there has been a proceeding *in rem*,[101] or, more specifically, *quasi in rem*.[102] That is to say, according to the meanings of the phrases *in personam* and *in rem* in this particular context, the proceedings from the beginning of the action down to and including the execution sale have a twofold aspect and effect: (1) the *primary stage* of the entire proceedings, ie, down to judgment, is, considered *by itself*, a proceeding *in personam*; (2) the primary stage *and* the secondary stage (from and after judgment) are, considered *together*, a proceeding *quasi in rem* with reference to the particular property sold in the execution sale.

Instead of suing B for damages and receiving a judgment *in personam*, as above described, A might in some jurisdictions, in case B be absent from the jurisdiction, attach a definite piece of B's property; and ultimately this might be sold to satisfy A's claim for damages. In this case the *entire* proceeding, since its only effect is to extinguish B's ownership of the very property attached (if any he had) and create new and corresponding ownership in the execution purchaser, is a proceeding *quasi in rem*.

It will thus be seen that, *even in the law courts*, the vindication of primary rights *in rem* may, according to the circumstances, be by proceedings *in personam*, or by proceedings *quasi in rem*, or by *both forms* of proceeding (primary and secondary stages of the ordinary action at law).[103] It is equally obvious that a primary right *in personam*, e.g. A's right that B pay him \$10,000, may frequently be vindicated only by an attachment proceeding, - i.e., one *quasi in rem*.

The point that the primary rights may be *in rem*, although the vindication proceedings are *in personam* in the special sense that such phrase has in the present context, is often brought out in admiralty cases. Thus: 1907, Mr Justice Holmes, in *The Hamilton*:

> We pass to the other branch of the first question: whether the state law, being valid, will be applied in the admiralty. Being valid, it

> *created an obligatio, a personal liability* of the owner of the Hamilton, *to the claimants. Slater* v *Mexican National R.R. Co*, 194 U.S., 120, 126. This, of course, the admiralty would not disregard, but would respect *the right* when brought before it in any legitimate way. *Ex parte McNeil*, 13 Wall., 236, 243. It might not give a *proceeding in rem*, since the statute does not purport to create a lien. It might give a *proceeding in personam*.[104]

Let us now suppose, in the Blackacre case, that instead of suing at law (after B has committed a destructive trespass), A secures from an equity court, *ab initio*, an injunction against B. The decree of the court here (end of 'primary stage' of the equitable proceeding) would result in imposing a (new) duty on B not to trespass on Blackacre; and, correlatively, A would have a (new) equitable right.[105] This first stage of the equitable proceeding would be *in personam* in the same general sense that the primary stage of the law court's is *in personam*. If B fails to fulfil the negative duty imposed by the injunction, there will ordinarily occur a 'secondary stage,' resulting in imprisonment for contempt. So far as this is said to be 'enforcement' or procedure *in personam*, it involves a *different* and *more literal* use of the phrase *in personam* than in any of the instances previously considered.[106] But the point for special emphasis here is that A's primary rights *in rem* are now being vindicated exclusively by equitable proceedings that are *in personam* in one sense so far as the primary stage is concerned and *in personam* in a different sense so far as the secondary stage is concerned.

On what possible ground, therefore, even assuming that equity could 'act only *in personam*,'[107] could it be said that for that reason there could be no equitable primary rights *in rem*, i.e., multital rights? If the usual legal proceedings were abolished, and A could vindicate his Blackacre rights *in rem* only in equity, would they thereby cease to be rights *in rem* and become only rights *in personam?*

Suppose, indeed, that we have a devise of Whiteacre to X for life, with remainder in fee to Y if, and only if, Y survives Z. Until Z's death before the death of X, Y has, obviously, only a contingent remainder. Let us assume, further, that T is threatening a destructive trespass to the premises, including the ruining of the mansion house. Y, the contingent remainderman, has no 'legal' rights *in rem*, for he has no *vested* rights, etc., but only 'possibilities' - ie, *potential* rights, privileges, etc.[108]

Has he not, however, actual, exclusively equitable rights *in rem*, that is, respective multital rights against T and other persons indiscriminately that they shall not seriously and permanently harm the land? There are numerous decisions to the effect that Y has an exclusively equitable right that the life tenant, X, shall not commit 'waste.' It is clear, also, that the reasons are equally great for recognizing *exclusively equitable rights* against *persons in general* that they shall not harm the land and defeat the 'legal' (i.e., concurrently legal and equitable) rights, privileges, etc., of the remainderman if his estate should ever vest 'in interest' and, ultimately, in 'possession and enjoyment,' - that is, exclusively equitable *multital* rights, or rights *in rem*. The *dicta* in the cases relating to waste afford strong support for this conclusion.[109] Similarly, suppose that J conveys the absolute legal title of Greenacre to K to secure a debt of $10,000, the agreement being that K is to be entitled to possession until the maturity of the debt and that when the debt is paid K is to reconvey the absolute legal title to J. While K is thus in possession, M threatens to cut down the ornamental trees on the place. If the threatened acts were committed, J would of course have no legal remedy, since the 'legal' rights *in rem* (ie, rights concurrently legal and equitable,[110] are now vested in K. It would, however, seem clear on principle that J is entitled to an injunction against M,[111] or, in other words, that J has exclusively equitable *multital* rights, or rights *in rem*, relating directly to the physical corpus of the property. The nature of the equitable rights, privileges, powers, and immunities of the *cestui que trust* is too large a subject for adequate treatment in the present place; and so any further consideration of that interesting subject must be reserved for another occasion.[112] It is hoped, however, that the various classes of rights and remedies already discussed are sufficient to show that the intrinsic nature of substantive primary rights - whether they be rights *in rem* or rights *in personam* - is not dependent on the character of the proceedings by which they may be vindicated.[113]

Notes

1 One of the chief purposes of the earlier article [Section 1] was to establish a firm foundation for the analysis and discussion of complex jural interests, or aggregates of jural relations, - the interest of the *cestui que* trust having been more especially in view. See above 21-23. This last-mentioned subject receives some incidental consideration in the pages following; but a more adequate treatment must be reserved for another occasion.

2 See above 30 where the individual conceptions represented in the scheme are treated at length.

3 See Mr Justice Holmes, 'The Path of the Law' (1897) 10 *Harvard Law Review* 456, 474-475:

> Jurisprudence, as I look at it, is simply law in its most generalized part. Every effort to reduce a case to a rule is an effort of jurisprudence, although the name as used in English is confined to the Broadest rules and most fundamental conceptions. One mark of a great lawyer is that he sees the application of the broadest rules. There is a story of a Vermont justice of the peace before whom a suit was brought by one farmer against another for breaking a churn. The justice took time to consider, and then said that he had looked through the statutes and could find nothing about churns, and gave judgment for the defendant. The same state of mind is shown in all our common digests and text-books. Applications of rudimentary rules of contract or tort are tucked away under the head of Railroads or Telegraphs or go to swell treatises on historical subdivisions, such as Shipping or Equity, or are gathered under an arbitrary title which is thought likely to appeal to the practical mind, such as Mercantile Law. If a man goes into law it pays to be a master of it, and to be a master of it means to look straight through all the dramatic incidents and to discern the true basis for prophecy. Therefore, it is well to have an accurate notion of what you mean by law, by a right, by a duty, by malice, intent, and negligence, by ownership, by possession, and so forth. I have in my mind cases in which the highest courts seem to me to have floundered because they had no clear ideas on some of these themes.

The following observations of the same learned judge are also deserving of consideration: 'As long as the matter to be considered is debated in artificial terms there is a danger of being led by a technical definition to apply a certain name, and then to deduce consequences which have no relation to the grounds on which the name was applied'. Mr Justice Holmes in *Guy* v *Donald* (1906) 203 US 399, 406; 27 Sup. Ct. Rep 63, 64 and: 'It is one of the misfortunes of the law that ideas become encysted in phrases and thereafter for a long time cease to provoke further analysis'. Mr Justice Holmes in *Hyde* v *United States* (1911) 225 US 347, 391.

Compare the remarks of Lord Kinnear in *Bank of Scotland* v *Macleod* [1914] AC 311, 324. He there endorses Lord Westbury's declaration that 'there is not a more fruitful source of error in law than the inaccurate use of language', and Lord Mansfield's observation that 'nothing in law is so apt to mislead as a metaphor'. The learned judge also remarks: 'The fallacy consists in using legal terms in a popular or metaphorical sense and yet affixing to them all the legal consequences which would attach to their use in a strictly technical sense'.

See also, as regards confusion of thought resulting from loose or ambiguous legal terms, Field J in *Morgan* v *Louisiana* (1876) 93 US 217, 223; and Peckham, J in *Phoenix Ins Co* v *Tennessee* (1895) 161 US 174, 177, 178.

[4] Owing, however, to limitations of space, it has proved necessary to exclude at this time a large part of the available illustrative material originally intended to be presented.

[5] For an explanation of the classification of jural relations as 'concurrent' and 'exclusive' see the writer's article entitled 'The Relations between Equity and Law' (1913) 11 *Michigan Law Review* 537, 553, 569.

See also the article of the writer's friend and colleague, Professor Walter Wheeler Cook, 'The Alienability of Choses in Action: A Reply to Professor Williston' (1917) 30 *Harvard Law Review* 449, 460 ff.

6 In this sentence the word 'formal' must not be ignored; for, in emphasizing for the time being the formal and analytical side of legal problems, the writer would not be thought to underestimate the great importance of other phases of the law, both scientific and practical. he has had occasion elsewhere to discuss more comprehensively the fundamental aspects of the law, including historical, or genetic, jurisprudence; comparative, or eclectic, jurisprudence; formal, or analytical, jurisprudence; critical, or teleological, jurisprudence; legislative, or constructive, jurisprudence; empirical, or functional, jurisprudence. See WN Hohfeld, 'A Vital School of Jurisprudence and Law' [1914] *Proceedings of the Association of American Law Schools for 1914* 76-139.

7 (1900) 175 Mass 71, 76.

8 (1915) 16 Ariz 540, 554.

9 (1915) 16 Ariz 540, 558.

10 Compare, as regards the significance and propriety of these terms, 'primary stage' and 'secondary stage' as applied to a suit in equity or an action at law, Lord Hardwicke in *Penn* v *Lord Baltimore* (1750) 1 Ves 444, 454:

> As to the court's not inforcing the execution of their judgment; if they could not at all, I agree, it would be in vain to make a decree; and that the court cannot inforce their own decree in rem, in the present case: but that is not an objection against making a decree in the cause; for the strict primary decree in this court as a court of equity is in personam, long before it was settled, whether this court could issue [sic] to put into possession in a suit of lands in England; which was first begun and settled in the time of James I. but ever since done by injunction or writ of assistant to the sheriff: but the court cannot to this day as to lands in Ireland or the plantations. In Lord King's time in the case of Richardson v Hamilton, Attorney General of Pennsylvania, which was a suit of land and a house in the town of Philadelphia, the court made a decree, though it could not be inforced in rem. In the case of Lord Anglesey of land lying in Ireland, I decreed for distinguishing and settling the parts of the estate, though impossible to inforce that decree in rem, but the party being in England, I could inforce it by process of contempt in personam and sequestration, which is the proper jurisdiction of this court.

It is interesting to observe that Lord Hardwicke speaks of the writ of assistance (under which an equity plaintiff might through the sheriff be put into actual possession of land) as a means by which a court of equity could at times 'enforce in rem' the 'strict primary decree *in personam*'.

11 For an able and search discussion of proceedings in personam and proceedings in rem, see the series of articles of Professor Walter Wheeler Cook entitled 'The Powers of Courts of Equity' (1915) 15 *Columbia Law Review* 37, 106, 228.

See also the present writer's article 'The Relations between Equity and Law' (1913) 11 *Michigan Law Review* 537 *passim*.

12 TE Holland, *Jurisprudence*, 10th edn (1906) 80-81.

Compare J Austin, *Jurisprudence*, 5th edn (1885) vol 1, 285-286 n, referring to the same ambiguity as Holland, and adding: 'Since the strongest and wariest minds are often ensnared by ambiguous words, their [the Germans'] confusion of those disparate objects is a venial error'.

Compare also *ibid* 322 n:

> In the language of English jurisprudence, facts or events which are contracts quasi or uti, are styled implied contracts, or contracts which the law implies: that is to say, contracts *quasi* or *uti*, and genuine though tacit contracts, are denoted by a common name, or by names nearly alike. And, consequently, contracts, *quasi* or *uti*, and implied or tacit contracts, are commonly or frequently confounded by English lawyers. See, in particular, Sir William Blackstone's *Commentaries*, (1765) bk 2, ch 30 and bk 3, ch9.

13 For judicial opinions recognizing the broad and generic significance of this term when loosely used, see the authorities discussed above 29-39.

Compare also, to similar effect, Slater J in *Shaw* v *Proffitt* (1910) 57 Or 192, 201:

> It is strenuously urged by defendant's counsel that, under the pleadings in this case, plaintiff stands on a bare parol license, which he claims to have obtained from the defendant and his predecessors in interest and that, therefore, plaintiff is precluded from obtaining the full effect of his evidence. We do not agree with such restricted interpretation of the language found in the complaint. It is averred that plaintiff obtained the 'right' as well as the 'consent, permission and license of defendant and his predecessors'. The word 'right' denotes, among other things, 'property,' 'interest,' 'power,' 'prerogative,' 'immunity,' and 'privilege,' and in law is most frequently applied to property in its restricted sense.

14 See above 30-31.

15 In this connection, the language of Mr Justice Stayton in *Mellinger* v *City of Houston* (1887) 68 Tex 37, 45; 3 SW 249, 253, though not recommended for precision, may well be compared:

> A right has been well defined to be a well-founded claim, and a well-founded claim means nothing more nor less than a claim recognized or secured by law ... Rights which pertain to persons, other than such as are termed natural rights, are essentially the creatures of municipal law, written or unwritten, and it must necessarily be held that a right, in a legal sense, exists, when in consequence of given facts the law declares that one person is entitled to enforce against another a claim .

16 The words 'group of persons' are intended to cover cases of so-called 'joint' rights and duties.

[Note by Cook: For a brief discussion of the concept of 'joint rights', see WW Cook, 'Hohfeld's Contributions to the Science of Law' (1919) 28 *Yale Law Journal* 721, 731-2.]

17 While the word 'paucital' is suggested as the generic term to cover all rights in personam, the word 'unital' would be available to denote that particular kind of right in personam that is 'unique' and 'uncompanioned'.

18 The reasons for including the words 'actual and potential' must be discussed at a later time, fater a genral consideration of the distinction between 'actual' and 'potential' jural relations.

19 It is not infrequently thought that the word 'general' is both appropriate and available to denote those rights, or claims, that are here called 'multital'. See, eg W Markby, *Elements of Law*, 6th edn (1905) sec 165. It is submitted, however, that according to the best usage the term 'general,' as applied to a jural relation, indicates that the latter is one of a large class of similar relations residing respectively in many persons, ie, people in general. For example, any duty correlating with a multitual right would be a general, or common, duty. The right of a person not to be struck by another is both multital and general.

This matter will receive more complete consideration at a later time.

20 Compare F Pollock and FW Maitland, *History of English Law*, 2d edn (1905) vol 2, 178.

21 It is sometimes assumed that rights *in rem* (considered collectively) are such only as avail against absolutely all persons, an idea fostered in part by the frequently used expression 'against all the world'. See, eg CC Langdell, *Summary of Equity Pleading*, 2nd edn (1883) sec 184; Langdell, 'A Brief Survey of Equity Jurisdiction' (1887) 1 *Harvard Law Review* 50; Hart, 'The Place of Trusts in Jurisprudence' (1912) 28 *Law Quarterly Review* 290, 296 and Terry, 'The Arrangement of the Law' (1917) 17 *Columbia Law Review* 365, 376. This notion is not warranted according to general usage. If, for example, A, the owner of Blackacre, has given his friends C and D 'leave and license' to enter, A has no rights against C and D that they shall not enter; but he has such rights against persons in general; and they are clearly to be classified as being 'multital' or '*in rem*'.

For further phases of this matter, see above n 157 and below 82-87.

Similarly, compare the rights, etc., of one wrongfully in possession: *Jeffries* v *Great Western Ry* (1856) 5 E and B 802 and *The Winkfield* (1902) p. 42.

22 As indicated by the examples given, multital rights are always constructive rather than concensual; that is, they are their correlating duties arise independently of even an approximate expression of intention on the part of those concerned. This explains, no doubt, why most, if not all, of such duties are negative in character: it is just and politic to spread such merely negative duties broadeast; whereas precisely the opposite would be true in the case of most kinds of affirmative duties.

23 (1915) 16 Ariz 540, 555.

Compare, for precisely similar language, J Austin, *Jurisprudence*, 5th edn (1885) vol 2, 957.

24 As to the prevalent and unfortunate tendency to confuse legal and non-legal conceptions, see the more general discussion above 23-27. See also below nn 168, 223.

25 (1900) 175 Mass 71, 76.

Compare also the following from *ibid* 77 per Mr Justice Holmes's opinion:

> It is true as an historical fact that these symbols are used in admiralty proceedings, and also, again merely as an historical fact, that the proceedings in rem have been confined to cases where certain classes of claims, although of very divers sorts, for indemnification for injury, for wages, for salvage, etc, are to be asserted. But a ship is not a person. It cannot do a wrong or make a contract. To say that a ship has committed a tort is merely a shorthand way of saying that you have decided to deal with it as if it had committed one, because some man has committed one in fact. There is no a priori reason why any other claim should not be enforced in the same way. If a claim for a wrong committed by a master may be enforced against all interests in the vessel, there is no juridical objectioin to a claim of title being enforced in the same way. The fact that it is not so enforced under existing practice affords no test of the powers of the Legislature. The contrary view would indicate that you really believed the fiction that a vessel had an independent personality as a fact behind the law'.

26 W Markby, *Elements of Law*, 6th edn (1905) sec 165.

To say that all rights, or claims, must avail against persons is, of course, simply another way of asserting that all duties must rest upon persons. The latter is no less obvious than the proposition that all rights must reside in persons.

Compare Mr Justice Markby *ibid* sec 163:

> The chief, in my opinion the only, use of a division of law into the law of persons and the law of things is as a convenient arrangement of topics in a treatise or a code. As used for this purpose I shall speak of it hereafter. But by slightly changing the terms in which this classification is expressed, Blackstone has introduced an important error, which it is desirable to notice here. He speaks not of the law of persons and of the law of things, but of rights of persons and of rights of things. Rights of persons there are undoubtedly; for all rights are such. There may be also rights over things, and rights over persons; but rights of, that is, belonging to, things, as opposed to rights of, that is, belonging to, persons, there cannot be.

Compare also Mr Justice Henshaw in *Western Indemnity Co* v *Pillsbury* (1915) 170 Cal 686, 719:

> Again it is said that it is thought expedient that the loss by injuries to workmen should be borne by the industries and not by the men. But this is only a euphemism which obscures the facts and darkens reason. It is like other happy catch-phrases that deceive the mind by pleasing the ear. We have many such. 'Putting the rights of property before the rights of men,' is one - as though property apart from those of its human owner, ever did or could have any rights. So that the rights of property are absolutely the rights of men.

27 The consideratioin being actually paid to B, the validity of B's promise to A is, of course, not subject to question merely because B was already under a similar duty to X.

28 See below 75-80.

29 *Law of Property in Land*, 1st edn (1874) 1, 2.

30 Beale, *Treatise on Conflict of Laws* (1916) sec 139. All will agree with Professor Beale that, for accurate thinking and correct results in the conflict of laws, it is of vital importance to have sound and consistent conceptions of legal rights and other jural relations; and it is evident that, pursuant ot this idea, much of the learned author's reasoning and very many of his arguments and conclusions on specific problems in the conflict of laws have, very naturally, been directly based on his 'preliminary survey' of 'rights' and on his supposed distinction between what he calls 'static rights' and what he calls 'dynamic rights,'

Yet it may be doubted whether Professor Beale has made clear and consistent his conception of a so-called 'static right' as 'a legally recognized interest in, to, or against a person or a thing'; and thus one is forced the more to question the validity of many of his arguments and conclusions in the closely related fields of jurisprudence and conflict of laws.

At one time the 'static right' seems to be a purely factual 'interest' existing independently of law; at another time a relation 'created by law'. The former idea is suggested when the learned author refers to Gareis's definition of 'interests'. This appears very clearly not only from the intrinsic meaning of Gareis's language as quoted by Professor Beale, but also from certain introductory words which are to be found in Gareis's original work: 'Interests, considered as facts, arise directly from egoism, and are nothing other than subjectively perceived relations,' etc. See Gareis. Systematic Survey (Kocourek's translation) 31. Indeed, Professor Beale himself, in the very definition quoted in the text of the present article, defines 'a right' as an 'interest,' not as some legal relation protecting the interest: there is a very obvious difference - and one vitally important for the solution of problems in the conflict of laws - between a mere factual interest and its legal recognition (legal claims, privileges, etc.).

In *ibid* sec 141, however, we find the following:

> A static right, or as it is commonly called a vested interest, is a legally protected interest in a person or thing. Such an interest is one which continues indefinitely, and protection of it therefore requires a right which, like the interest it protects, has the character of permanence. Accordingly a static right remains in existence until either the subject of the interest ceases to exist or the law itself by a special act puts an end to the right'.

In this passage we are told first, that a 'static right' is an interest; second, that the 'right' is something other than 'the interest it protects'; third, that 'a static right remains in existence until ... the law itself ... puts an end to the right'.

A similar sudden and difficult shift seems to occur in sec 142. Thus:

> A static right, as has been seen, is the interest of a person in a thing or in a person; the right is created by law, and once created it is permanent, that is, it persists until the proper law puts an end to it. The law that creates it, as will be seen, also provides for its preservation, by creating a hedge of protecting

> rights about it; rights of the owner or possessor to have it free from interference or destruction … It is to be regarded as a legal entity quite apart from the particular protection with which it may be endued by law.

31 *Modern Law of Real Property* (1903) sec 273.

32 See EW Huffcut, *The Law of Agency*, ed, 2nd edn (1901) sec 10.

33 (1828) 3 Russ, 1, 22, 24.

34 (1857) 43 Me 578, 587.

35 The pair of terms, '*jus in personam*' and '*jus in rem*', as contrasted with the pair of terms, '*actio in personam*' and '*actio in rem*', was not in general use among the Roman jurists. Compare E C Clark, *History of Roman Private Law: Jurisprudence* (1914) vol. 2, 711: '*Jus in rem* and *Jus in re* in Roman Law. The former of these expressions is very little used by the Roman Jurists, but, in the few passages in which is occurs, *res* clearly means the thing itself as distinguished, eg from its value. See Ulpian, *Digest* 32, 20: '*Nullum quidem jus in ipsam rem habere, sed actionem de pretio*'. Cf J E Goudsmit, *The Pandects* (1873) 247 n'

It is clear, therefore, that the 'all-pervading and important' Roman law distinction to which Austin refers was that represented by *obligatio* and *dominium*. Compare J Austin, *Jurisprudence*, 5th edn (1885) vol. 1, 383:

> By *jus in rem* and *jus in personam*, the authors of those terms intended to indicate this broad and simple distinction; which the Roman lawyers also marked by the words *dominium* and *obligatio* - terms the distinction between which was the groundwork of all their attempts to arrange rights and duties in an accurate or scientific manner.

Also *ibid* vol. 2, 773:

> The first great distinction among primary rights has been very fully explained in a preceding part of this Course. I allude to the distinction between dominia and obligationes, as they were called by the classical jurists; between jura in rem and jura in personam, as they have been styled by modern Civilians.

36 *Ibid* vol. 1, 369, 370.

37 W Markby, *Elements of Law*, 6th edn (1905) sec 165.

38 (1883) 105 Ill 364, 379.

39 (1886) 143 Mass 538.

40 (1903) 194 US 601, 606.

41 (1904) 195 US 375, 382.

42 (1905) 197 US 544, 575.

43 [1913] AC 76, 85.

44 [1914] AC 398, 418, 419.

45 [1914] AC 398, 458.

46 (1916) 242 US 171, 177; 37 Sup Ct Rep 34, 35.

47 That is, if A has a right in personam against B that the latter shall 'transfer' some 'legal

interest,' e.g. title of Blackacre, to A, A is said to have only a *jus ad rem*; whereas after conveyance made by B, A would have *jus in re*.

For very interesting instances of the use of the terms *jus in re* and *jus ad rem* in connection with attempts to explain the nature of uses and trusts, see F Bacon, *Uses* (circa 1602) Rowe's edn (1806) 5-6 and E Coke, *First Part of the Institutes of the Laws of England* (1628) sec 464. Both of these passages are quoted above, sec 1, nn 1, 2.

48 W Markby, *Elements of Law*, 6th edn (1905) 99 n.

49 [1914] AC 398, 431.

50 [1914] AC 311, 324.

51 (1855) 2 Curtis 404, 406, 410, 411, 412, 414.

52 (1900) 177 US 655, 666.

53 (1870) 50 NH 71, 75.

54 History of Roman Law: Jurisprudence (1914) vol. 2, 718.

55 (1855) 2 Curtis, 404, 412.

56 [1914] AC 311, 324.

57 See the quotations given above: Mr Justice Holmes, 83-84; Mr Justice Brandeis, 85; Lord Sumner, 84.

See also the term 'personal rights' as used by Mr Justice Holmes, dissenting, in the very recent case of *Southern Pacific Co* v *Jensen* (1917) 244 US 205; 37 Sup Ct 524.

58 See below 53-54.

59 *Jurisprudence*, 5th edn (1885) vol. 1, 368, 394, 371, 586.

60 W Markby, *Elements of Law*, 6th edn (1905) 91, 99.

61 *Jurisprudence*, 10th edn (1906) 139.

62 JW Salmond, *Jurisprudence*, 4th edn (1913) 202, 203.

63 Law and Its Administration (1915) 53.

64 (1916) 30 *Harvard Law Review* 97, 98.

65 See also the various judicial opinions from which quotations are given immediately above.

66 Compare, however, special cases like *Thorpe* v *Brumfitt* (1873) LR 8 Ch App 650, involving a suit for an injunction against several defendants for disturbance of plaintiff's right of way. Lord Justice James said:

> The plaintiff cannot complain, unless he can prove an obstruction which injures him. The case is not like one of trespass, which gives a right of action though no damage be proved. In the present case, I cannot come to any other conclusion than that arrived at by the Master of the Rolls, that the right of access to the inn-yard has been interfered with in a way most prejudicial to the Plaintiff. Nothing can be much more injurious to the owner of an inn than that the way to his yard should be constantly obstructed by the loading and unlaoding of heavy waggons. If a person who was going to put up his horses at the inn was stopped by the loading or unloading of waggons, he would probably at once go to another inn. Then it was said that the Plaintiff alleges an obstruction caused by several persons acting independently of each other, and does not shew what share each had in causing it. It is probably impossible for a person in the Plaintiff's position to shew this. Nor do I think it necessary that he should shew it. The amount of obstruction

> caused by any one of them might not, if it stood alone, be sufficient to give any ground of complaint, though the amount caused by them all may be give any ground of complaint, though the amount caused by them all may be a serious injury. Suppose one person leaves a wheelbarrow standing on a way, that may cause no appreciable inconveniences, but if a hundred do so, that may cause a serious inconvenience, which a person entitled to the use of the way has a right to prevent; and it is no defence to any one person among the hundred to say that what he does causes of itself no damage to the complainant.

67 Some would say yes: compare Sir Frederick Pollock, *Jurisprudence*, 2nd edn (1904) 64:

> Doubtless there are duties without any determinate rights corresponding to them: indeed, this is the case, in any view, with the negative duties which we owe to the community at large. For my duty not to damage other people's goods, for example, is one duty, not millions of separate duties owed to every one who has anything to be damaged, or in respect of every separate chattel of any value'.

68 (1908) 147 NC 142, 146.

69 [1906] 2 KB 627, 638.

70 See above 24-26, 48. Compare also Mr Justice Foster in *Pullitzer* v *Livingston* (1896) 89 Me 359: 'With all the rights, privilege, and powers incident to ownership, etc'. See also Professor Arthur L Corbin, 'Offer and Acceptance, and Some of the Resulting Legal Relations' (1917) 26 *Yale Law Journal* 172.

71 (1874) LR 9 Ch App 221, 223.
Compare Henry Pitney VC in *Hennessy* v *Carmony* (1892) 50 NJ Eq 616.

72 *Jurisprudence*, 5th edn (1885) vol 1, 397, vol 2, 799, 802, 808.

73 *Ibid* vol 1, 395.

74 It is, of course, possible for a given writer to 'impose' on a term what meaning he will, within the principle of the following: 'When I use a word,' Humpty Dumpty said, in rather a scornful tone, 'it means just what I choose it to mean, neither more nor less'. 'The question is,' said Alice, 'whether you can make words mean so many different things'. 'The question is,' said Humpty Dumpty, 'which is to be the master! That's all'. L Carroll, *Through the Looking Glass* (1891) ch 4.

If, however, this more or less arbitrary plan be pursued, it is at least desirable that it be done premeditatedly, and that adequate notice be given. It is, moreover, believed that, in the cases put in the text, the difficulties involved are concerned primarily with concepts rather than terms.

75 W Markby, *Elements of Law*, 6th edn (1905) 98.

76 *Elements of Jurisprudence*, 10th edn (1906) 139.

77 JW Salmond, *Jurisprudence*, 4th edn (1913) 202, 203.

78 *Law of Property in Land*, 1st edn (1874) 2.

79 (1887) 1 *Harvard Law Review* 1, 9.

80 *Law and Its Administration* (1915) 51, 54, 57.

81 (1916) 30 *Harvard Law Review* 97, 98.

82 (1904) 194 US 120, 125.

83 (1900) 175 Mass 71, 76.

84 (1890) 3 *Harvard Law Review* 23, 25, 28, 29, 30, 31, 33, 34, 337.

85 Compare *ibid* 313 *passim*; consider especially the statement (314): 'A true property may, therefore, be shortly defined as possession coupled with the unlimited right of possession'. This definition would seem to involve a serious confusion of physical relations with legal relations.

Compare also JB Ames, *Lectures on Legal History* (1913) 76, passage quoted below 86.

86 See *ibid* 60 n 1, 178 ff.

For judicial consideration of the early history of the action of trespass, see *Admiralty Commissioners* v *SS Amerika* [1917] AC 38.

87 [Note by Cook: Compare Cook, 'Powers of Courts of Equity' (1915) 15 *Columbia Law Review* 37, 45.]

88 All legal rights, if genuine and valid, are really 'concurrently legal and equitable,' if considered with respect to the sanctions involved. See WN 'The Relations between Equity and Law (1913) 11 *Michigan Law Review* 537 and also Professor Walter Wheeler Cook, 'The Alienability of Choses in Action: A Reply to Professor Williston' (1917) 30 *Harvard Law Review* 449, 455.

89 Compare Viscount Haldane LC in *Sinclair* v *Brougham* [1914] AC 398, 418, 419, quoted above 63.

90 Compare Lord Justice Cozens-Hardy in *Capital and Counties Bank Ltd* v *Rhodes* [1903] 1 Ch 655-656:

> The transfer by registered disposition takes effect by virtue of an overriding power, and not by virtue of any estate in the registered proprietor ... Notwithstanding tha the land has become registered land it may still be dealt with by deeds having the same operation and effect as they would have if the land were unregistered, subject only to the risk of the title being defeated ... by the exercise of the statutory powers of disposition given to the registered proprietor, against which the mortagee must protect himself by notice on the register'.

91 *Summary of Equity Pleading*, 2nd edn (1883) sec 184.

92 (1900) 13 *Harvard Law Review* 673, 677. For analysis and criticism of the views of Professors Langdell, Ames, and Maitland as regards the relations of substantive equitable doctrines to substantive legal doctrines, see the present writer's article, 'The Relations between Equity and Law' (1913) 11 *Michigan Law Review* 537.

See also WN Hohfeld, 'Supplemental Note on The Conflict of Equity and Law' (1916-7) 26 *Yale Law Journal* 767.

93 For criticism of this assumption, see above n 159.

94 But see Holmes J in *Tyler* v *Court of Registration* (1900) 175 Mass 71, 76, quoted post n 236.

95 *Lectures on Legal History* (1913) 76. Compare Professor Harlan F Stone, *Law and Its Administration* (1915) 93, 95:

> Since a judgment at law affects only the property of the parties to the litigation, it is sometimes spoken of as a judgment *in rem*. The weakness, as well as the strength of such a system of procedure is apparent. To avail one's self of a legal remedy, one must wait until his rights have been interfered with and he has suffered some legal damage ... The distinguishing feature of equity is that the chancellor, or equity judge, who, because of his official position, originally had delegated to him the royal prerogative of command, has power to command things to be done or not to be done. That is, the equity courts act in personam, as it is said, or against the person, as distinguished from the law courts whose jurisdiction is in rem or over the property of the litigants. Thus, the chancellor could enjoin the defendant from committing a threatened injury of the plaintiff's property, or make a decree directing the defendant to convey property to the plaintiff in accordance with his contract. If the defendant failed to obey, he could be punished for contempt by imprisonment until he became obedient to the court.

96 *Collected Papers* (1911) vol 3, 321, 350 n 1.

97 See above 81.

98 See Mr Justice Holmes, in *Tyler* v *Court of Registration* (1900) 175 Mass 71, 76:

> If the technical object of the suit is to establish a claim against some particular person, with a judgment which generally, in theory at least, binds his body ... the action is in personam, although it may concern the right to or possession of a tangible thing.

See also a later passage in the learned judge's opinion (77) referring to a judgment *in personam* as one establishing 'an infinite personal liability'.

99 See AC Freeman, *A Treatise of the Law of Judgments*, 4th edn (1898) secs 432 ff.

100 As regards 'the primary stage' and 'the secondary stage' of an action at law or suit in equity, compare Lord Hardwicke in *Penn* v *Lord Baltimore* (1750) 1 Ves 444, 454, quoted above n 148 .

101 Even though such execution sale take place as a result of, and subsequent to, a judgment for money, neither the action brought to secure such a judgment nor the judgment itself, is said to be *in rem*. (Cf, however, Professor Ames, above 86 and Professor Stone above n 233.) On the contrary, both the action and the judgment are said to be *in personam*. See Mr Justice Holmes in *Tyler* v *Court of Registration* (1900) 175 Mass 71, 76, quoted above n 236.

See also Mr Justice Cutting in *Redington* v *Frye* (1857) 43 Me 578, 586:

> And the embarrassment has arisen in a great measure by an erroneous idea that the remedy of the contractor and his sub-contractor is the same; whereas the former has his security on the goods and estate of his debtor, that is, in personam, as well as on the specific property benefited by his labor, which may be in rem, and after judgment it is optional with the creditor on which species of property he will levy his execution ... But a sub-contractor has no

> claim against the owner of the property - his claim is only against the property (in rem) and the person and property of his employer (*in personam*).

It is believed, however, that it tends greatly to clarify matters to distinguish sharply, as already indicated, the *two stages* of the judicial proceedings; for the two taken together operate, as regards such property as is sold on execution, just as if such property had been attached ab initio and subsequently sold, with no intermediate judgment *in personam* at all. Such an attachment proceeding would, of course, be called a proceeding *in rem*, or, more specifically, *quasi in rem*.

102 Compare Mr Justice Franklin in *Hook* v *Hoffman* (1915) 16 Ariz 540, 557:

> While, properly speaking, actions or proceedings *in rem* are against the thing itself, and for the purpose of disposing thereof without reference to the title of particular claimants, the term has in a larger and broader sense been applied to certain actions and proceedings between parties, where the object is to reach and dispose of property owned by them or in which they have an interest; but, as these are not strictly *in rem*, they have frequently and more properly been termed *quasi in rem*, or in the nature of actions or proceedings *in rem*.

It is, of course, inaccurate to describe the proceeding strictly in rem as one which is 'against the thing itself'. See Mr Justice Holmes in *Tyler* v *Court of Registration* (1900) 175 Mass 71, 77: 'Personification and naming the res as defendant are mere symobols, not the essential matter. They are fictions, conveniently expressing the nature ofl the process and the result, nothing more'.

It is submitted, moreover, that the distinction between a proceeding strictly *in rem* and one *quasi in rem* is not correctly or adequately described by saying that the former is against all the world and the latter against only a particular person. When, eg a vessel is sold, in an admiralty proceeding strictly in rem, the effect is to extingusih the ownership (ie, aggregate of rights, etc) of the owner and to vest a new and corresponding ownership in the pruchaser. So also, when a horse supposedly belonging to B, a judgment debtor, is sold by the sheriff under a writ of execution, a precisely similar result occurs, provided that B, the particular judgment debtor named, actually does own the horse. The proceeding strictly in rem is sure to 'hit the right target'; whereas the proceeding *quasi in rem* is not certain to do so.

The former, indeed, can be correctly and adequately understood only if it be realized that it is essentially an anonymous proceeding, being aimed to reach the interest of the true owner (or owners) of the property whoever he may be. The proceeding *quasi in rem* is, on the other hand, aimed to reach only the interest of a named party. The effect, therefore, so far as transfer of ownership is concerned, is necessarily conditional upon some legal interest being actually vested in the particular party named.

If effective, however, the ordinary proceeding *quasi in rem*, like that strictly *in rem*, affects the jural relations of all persons, not merely those of the present owner; for in each case the 'transfer of title' involves, as regards all persons, the extinguishment of their duties to the present owner in respect to the particular object involved and the creation of new and corresponding duties to the new owner.

103 Of course, even where a judgment *in personam* is sought, property may be attached *ab initio* and subsequently sold to satisfy the judgment.

104 (1907) 207 US 398, 405.

105 Compare *Fall* v *Eastin* (1909) 215 US 1, 14-15 (concurring opinion of Holmes J); *Mallette* v *Carpenter* (1916) 160 NW (Wis) 182. See the extended comment in (1917) 26 *Yale Law Journal* 311.

See also WN Hohfeld, 'The Relations between Equity and Law' (1913) 11 *Michigan Law Review* 537, 567-568.

106 For a summary of the different uses of the pair of phrases, *in personam* and *in rem*, see above 69-70.

For a comparison of imprisonment in an action at law, under a *capias ad respondendum* or *capias ad satisfaciendum*, with imprisonment for contempt in a chancery suit, for the purpose of coercing performance of a decree, see the thorough discussion by Professor Walter Wheeler Cook, 'The Powers of Courts of Equity' (1915) 15 *Columbia Law Review* 108 ff.

See also WN Hohfeld, 'The Relations between Equity and Law' (1913) 11 *Michigan Law Review* 537, 564-567.

107 Such an assumption itself seems to be inaccurate and misleading in view of the power of a court of equity to issue writs of assistance and writs of sequestration. See Lord Hardwicke in *Penn* v *Lord Baltimore* (1750) 1 Ves 444, 454, quoted above n 148. The learned judge there refers to a proceeding under a writ of assistance as a means by which the 'strict primary decree *in personam*' of a court of equity could sometimes be 'enforced *in rem*'.

Consider also the power of a court of equity to proceed [*quasi*] *in rem* in mortgage foreclosure cases: extinguishment of the 'equity of redemption'. Cf. *Paget* v *Ede* (1874) LR 18 Eq 118.

108 This statement should, in strictness, be qualifed.

Even at common law the contingent remainderman had the actual, or present, legal power to 'release' his interest to the owner of the estate in possession. The power to devise, and the power to make a so-called 'equitable assignment' should also be considered.

Very genrally the contingent remainderman now has, as a result of statute, the present legal power to alienate his potential interest *inter vivos*.

109 Compare the following statements from judicial opinions: Mr Justice Battle in *Braswell* v *Morehead* (1852) 45 NC 26, 28: 'Owners of executory bequests, and other contingent interests, stand in a position, in this respect, similar to vested remaindermen, and have a similar right to the protective jurisdiction of the Court' (ie, court of chancery); Mr Justice Connor in *Latham* v *Roanoke, etc Co* (1905) 51 SE (NC) 780: 'The interest of a contingent remainderman in the timber will be protected by a court of equity by injunction' and Mr Justice Shaw in *Pavkovitch* v *Southern Pacific R Co* (1906) 150 Cal 39, 50: 'The plaintiff's interest is not vested (*Civ. Code*, secs. 693, 695); and hence he has no present property in the rock removed, for the value of which damages can be computed, or to which he could have the right of present possession ... But the rule is different interest may protect that interest against deterioration or destruction by enjoining a threatened waste'.

110 For the classification of jural relations as 'concurrently legal and equitable' and 'exclusively equitable,' see WN Hohfeld, 'The Relations between Equity and Law' (1913) 11 *Michigan Law Review* 537.

111 *Smith* v *Collyer* (1803) 8 Ves 89, seems to have been such a case. The injunction was, to be sure, refused by Lord Eldon, - solely on the ground, however, that at that time bills to enjoin a 'trespass' as distinguished from 'waste' had not yet been definitely sanctioned by the court. Counsel for plaintiff argued: 'The plaintiffs have no means of preventing or redressing this at law, the mortgagee having the legal title; and the mischief will be irremediable'. Lord Eldon replied: 'I do not recollect any instance of this sort ... It is not waste, but trespass by their own showing. There was no instance of an injuction in trespass till the case before Lord Thurlow upon a mine; to which I have alluded; which, though trespass, was very near waste. In that case, the first instance of granting an injunction in trespass, there was no dispute whatsoever about the right. Here the right is disputed'.

See also Mr Justice Brewer in *Wilson* v *Rockwell* (1886) 29 Fed 674:

> The facts stated in the bill give complainants a clear right to a preliminary injunction. It is immaterial whether the legal title be in complainants or the Woodmass of Alston Company. The dispute between them does not concern trespassers. Both parties are in court, the company being made defendant. The full equitable title or ownership is with complainants, and a court of equity will protect the owners, as aginast trespassers, although the location of the legal title has not been finally determined.

In such a case as that relating to mortagor and mortgagee, the situation is not fundamentally different from that of *In re Nisbet and Potts' Contract* [1906] 1 Ch 386 - a case indicating that the equitable beneficiary of a restrictive agreement relating to land (sometimes called an 'equitable easement') has rights even against wrongful possessors, or disseisors, of the 'servient' land that they shall not act contrary to the terms of the restrictive agreement. In the latter case, as in that of the mortgagor and mortgagee, the legal owner of the land on which the acts of the defendant are done is not the equitable 'agent' or 'guardian' of the equitable beneficiary; and hence the grounds are peculiarly strong for giving to the equitable beneficiary direct equitable rights against all persons in respect to the physical corpus.

112 See WN Hohfeld, 'The Relations between Equity and Law' (1913) 11 *Michigan Law Review* 537, where the writer has sought to analyze most of the elements comprised in the interest of a *cestui que trust*.

See also WN Hohfeld, 'Supplemental Note on the Conflict of Equity and Law' (1916-7) 26 *Yale Law Journal* 767.

113 Compare F Bacon, *Uses* (circa 1602) Rowe's edn (1806) 5-6: 'So that *usus and status, sive possessio, potius differunt secundum rationem fori, quam secundum naturam rei,* for that one of them is in court of law, the other in court of conscience'.

Compare also Lord Dunedin in *Nocton* v *Ashburton* [1914] AC 932, 964:

> And then there are the duties which arise from a relatiionship without the intervention of contract in the ordinary sense of the term, such as the duties of a trustee to his cestui que trust or of a guardian to his ward. It is in this

latter class of cases that equity has been peculiarly dominant, not, I take it, from any scientific distinction between the classes of duty existing and the breaches thereof, but simply because in certain cases where common justice demanded a remedy, the common law had none forthcoming, and the common law (though there is no harder lesson for the stranger jurist to learn) began with the remedy and ended with the rights.

Index

For Product Safety Concerns and Information please contact our EU representative GPSR@taylorandfrancis.com
Taylor & Francis Verlag GmbH, Kaufingerstraße 24, 80331 München, Germany

www.ingramcontent.com/pod-product-compliance
Ingram Content Group UK Ltd.
Pitfield, Milton Keynes, MK11 3LW, UK
UKHW022122190926
475702UK00013B/1596

Mathematical Modelling for Engineering and Physical Applications

This edited volume from mathematical modelling experts employs a structured approach to showcase the latest research and provide a comprehensive guide to the principles, techniques and practical applications of mathematical modelling in the fields of engineering and the physical sciences.

Readers will gain an insight into the fundamentals of mathematical modelling, its application in engineering and the physical sciences, recent advances in the field, real-world case studies and challenges and future directions in the field. The book first introduces readers to the fundamentals of mathematical modelling, including the definition, scope and steps involved in the modelling process. Mathematical tools and techniques relevant to modelling are explained. The book then addresses the application of mathematical modelling in engineering and the physical sciences. It covers various domains, such as mechanical, biomedical, chemical, computer and environmental engineering, as well as green energy, physics and other physical science applications. Furthermore, the book explores the integration of data-driven approaches, leveraging the power of big data and analytics to enhance modelling capabilities. Through real-life case studies, readers gain practical insights into how mathematical modelling is applied in various industries and scientific disciplines. These case studies analyse the modelling process, challenges faced and outcomes achieved. Readers will gain a solid foundation to develop effective mathematical models and apply them to solve complex engineering and physical problems. This foundation will also enable them to tackle problems and make informed decisions in their own projects. Finally, readers will be able to anticipate and adapt to evolving technologies and stay ahead in their respective fields.

This book is a valuable resource primarily for undergraduate and graduate students seeking a comprehensive guide to this important discipline. Researchers, engineers and scientists will also benefit from the discussions within. Overall, the book empowers readers with the knowledge, skills and practical insights to effectively apply mathematical modelling in engineering and the physical sciences.